prices and incomes policy. the austrian experience

by

Dr. Hannes Suppanz

and

Mr. Derek Robinson

ORGANISATION FOR ECONOMIC CO-OPERATION AND DEVELOPMENT

The Organisation for Economic Co-operation and Development (OECD) was set up under a Convention signed in Paris on 14th December, 1960, which provides that the OECD shall promote policies designed:

— *to achieve the highest sustainable economic growth and employment and a rising standard of living in Member countries, while maintaining financial stability, and thus to contribute to the development of the world economy;*

— *to contribute to sound economic expansion in Member as well as non-member countries in the process of economic development;*

— *to contribute to the expansion of world trade on a multilateral, non-discriminatory basis in accordance with international obligations.*

The Members of OECD are Australia, Austria, Belgium, Canada, Denmark, Finland, France, the Federal Republic of Germany, Greece, Iceland, Ireland, Italy, Japan, Luxembourg, the Netherlands, Norway, Portugal, Spain, Sweden, Switzerland, Turkey, the United Kingdom and the United States.

CONTENTS

PREFACE

During 1970 a number of Member countries of OECD began to evince increasing concern over the rate of price rises and the Secretariat made renewed efforts, through a number of activities and studies, towards improving understanding of the causes and consequences of inflation. As a contribution and as one of the activities in the OECD's Labour-Management Programme, a multinational study group visited Austria to examine that country's prices and incomes policy and practice. The experience, since the last war, of many Member countries of a formal structure to incomes policy had proved somewhat disappointing but Austria, which has eschewed what seemed to be more overt and formal aspects had had a relatively successful record. It was considered useful, therefore, that Member countries with a different experience should have an opportunity of studying the institutional arrangements and operation and of confronting their hosts with the kind of problems which preoccupied them.

The group was composed of high level trade union and employer participants from Canada, Finland, Ireland, the Netherlands and the United Kingdom. Government observers from some of these countries also attended. The list of participants and programme are given in Annex.

The discussions of the group were chaired jointly by Mr. Friedrich Klau, Head of Division in the OECD Economic and Statistics Department, and Mr. Derek Robinson of the Oxford University Institute of Statistics and Economics and Fellow of Magdalen College.

The Austrian hosts spared no effort to give the visitors a very thorough insight into the operation of what would appear to be a unique system and every opportunity to question and discuss with a correspondingly high-level participation from their own side. The OECD would like to express its appreciation to all those who were responsible for ensuring the success of the visit and particularly to Federal Secretary of State Veselsky. The visit proved so stimulating that it was subsequently decided, exceptionally, to commission a special report on the Austrian experience, which it was hoped, would offer a valuable contribution to the debate on inflation.

This report has been prepared jointly by Dr. Hannes Suppanz, of the Osterreichisches Institut für Wirtschaftsforschung, and Mr. Derek Robinson. Parts I and II, which have been contributed by Dr. Suppanz, describe the institutional framework and assess the economic performance of the country during the period of the operation of prices and incomes policy. Part III, contributed by Mr. Robinson, is an evaluation in terms particularly of the social and political climate, by an outsider, but with considerable experience of incomes policy in his own country. The opinions are those of the authors alone and do not necessarily reflect those of either the OECD or the Austrian authorities.

Part I

THE INSTITUTIONAL FRAMEWORK

by

Dr. Hannes Suppanz

ECONOMIC AND SOCIAL BACKGROUND

Even before the Second World War prices and wages in Austria were from time to time controlled by the State and by bodies representing economic interests, but Austrian prices and incomes policy in its present form grew up in the post-war period and can only be understood when seen against this historical background. After the war the Austrian economy was largely destroyed and the GNP stood at only about a third of its pre-war figure (the 1938 level was not restored until 1949). When the wartime wages and prices freeze was relaxed, an inflationary spiral started and gathered speed, threatening to undermine reconstruction.

Faced with this difficult situation the two major parties, of almost equal strength, decided to bury their ideological differences and tackle the task of reconstruction in a spirit of compromise. Their joint experience of the civil war and political persecution, followed by a foreign occupation, had created a favourable climate for co-operation. In addition, co-operation between the two political camps was facilitated by close personal relations between the Government, the Parties (from 1945 to 1966 there was a "grand coalition" between the two major parties), and the influential centralized bodies representing economic interests.

The highly developed pre-war network of powerful unified bodies representing economic interests was completed by the creation of central organisations (a Federal Chamber of Trade and Industry was set up) and the merging of the sectional trade unions into one unified trade union. Almost all these bodies have regional branches and many are in addition subdivided by function and trade, but as a rule they are under strong central control. An organisation of such a kind enables close contact to be maintained with members whilst ensuring that their economic and political interests are effectively represented. The political thrust of these bodies is reinforced by the high degree of unionisation compared with other countries; two-thirds of all employed persons are covered by the Trade Union Federation and about 85% of all workers in private industry work for employers who belong to the Federation of Austrian Industry. Almost all workers and employers are legally obliged to be members of their respective Chambers.

The Chambers of Labour (Arbeiterkammern) embrace all persons in dependent employment and their top organisation is the Chambers of Labour Conference (Arbeiterkammertag), it having been decided not to have a Federal Chamber and instead to enlarge the Vienna Chamber. The Chamber is manned by a staff of qualified experts advising internal policy committees dealing with labour law, social insurance, price policy, statistics, etc. The Chambers of Agriculture (Landwirtschafts- kammern), headed by a Presidents' Conference, have many local bran- ches and in two of the Länder they also represent workers' interests, while in the other Länder there are separate Chambers of Farm Labour. For trade and industry a separate Federal Chamber was set up in addi- tion to the Land Chambers; like the latter it is subdivided into depart- ments and trade groupings. As membership of the Chambers is compul- sory, they have to find a compromise between the interests of their members. In addition to the representation of the interests of their members the Chambers also exercise certain central government func- tions, for example, they sit on the Agricultural Fund (Agrarfonds) Management Board (a part of the Agricultural market organisation) and are members of the official Price Commission. They have the right to criticize draft legislation and regulations and they sit on a large num- ber of advisory boards (Beiräte). The Chambers also have the impor- tant privilege of concluding collective agreements (other bodies only have this privilege if it is expressly granted to them).

Along with the comprehensive network of Chambers there are almost equally comprehensive arrangements for representing economic interests through bodies with voluntary membership, the most important of which are the Trade Union Federation and the Federation of Austrian Industry. There are close personal links between the bodies which represent the same members (between Chambers of Labour and Trade Unions, be- tween Chambers of Trade and Industry and the Federation of Austrian Industry) and also some degree of work-sharing (e. g. the Chambers of Labour do most of the economic and social research work on the work- ers' side). The major voluntary bodies (in particular the Trade Union Federation) have succeeded in acquiring much the same rights of co- determination and consultation as can legally be claimed only by the Chambers.

After the war the four major bodies representing economic interests (the Federal Chamber of Trade and Industry, the Chambers of Agriculture, the Chambers of Labour and the Trade Union Federation) acquired a considerable voice in economic policy; in 1947 they formed the "Economic Commission" with the function of watching economic developments and formulating proposals on remedial measures for submission to the Government. Between 1947 and 1951 five "prices and wages agreements" to combat inflation were concluded under the auspices of the "Economic Commission" and then given legal effect by Government and Parliament. An attempt to legalize co-operation between the Government and both sides of industry by setting up an "Economic Directorate" failed (it would have comprised members of the Government and the President of the National Bank, as well as the four major economic bodies), because the Court for the Protection of the Constitution ruled that such a body would be incompatible with ministerial responsibility.

Another feature of the Austrian economy which, along with the strong position of the organisations representing economic interests, has doubtless made it easier to operate a prices and incomes policy is the size of the public sector compared with other countries. In 1946 and 1947 the parliamentary parties unanimously agreed to nationalize electricity, further sectors of industry (mainly raw materials industries, but also important engineering, vehicle and electrical industries and the chemical industry) and money and credit institutions (the three main banks). About 30% of all persons in dependent employment work in the public sector and it contributes about 20% of the GNP. About two-thirds of the original capital of all Austrian share companies is owned directly or indirectly (e. g. through nationalized banks) by public authorities.

WAGE DETERMINATION

On the workers' side collective agreements are almost all concluded by the Trade Union Federation (with the sole exception of agricultural and forestry workers in certain Länder), because the Chamber of Labour does not assert its right to conclude collective agreements. The Austrian Trade Union Federation has a highly centralized structure subdivided mainly by groups of industries. Only one of the sixteen of its member Unions, the Private Employees' Union, covers all sectors of the economy (with the exception of the civil service and the liberal professions). The individual Trade Unions are further subdivided by region and trade down to plant level, but the Trade Union Headquarters are responsible for administration and financial control. Wage negotiations can also be conducted by subordinate trade union bodies, but agreements must be signed by the appropriate Trade Unions as the bodies duly authorized by the Federation.

The Trade Unions' firm foundations at plant level and the smooth flow of information between headquarters and branch organisations are partly due to the organisational structure; the works councils and shop stewards elected in plants become (if they belong to a Trade Union) junior officials of the Union under the terms of the statutes of the Trade Union Federation. The high degree of unionisation is also important. The Austrian Trade Union Federation has $1\frac{1}{2}$ million members, which is two-thirds of all persons in dependent employment. As those employment in the tertiary sector and in agriculture are difficult to unionise, this means that unionisation is almost complete in many branches of industry and the civil service.

On the employers' side the negotiating partner is usually a regional and/or departmental branch of the Federal Chamber of Trade and Industry, but this Chamber does not hold such a monopoly position as the Trade Union Federation does on the workers' side, since there are also other Chambers on the employers' side (the Chambers of Agriculture and the Liberal Professions Chambers), and the Federal Chamber of Trade and Industry leaves wage negotiations in some cases to voluntary groupings (e.g. to the Central Association of Graphic Trades). Although the Federation of Austrian Industry is empowered to conclude collective agreements, it does not assert its right. The Federal Chamber of Trade and Industry has set up "Labour Relations Committees" (arbeitsrechtliche Ausschüsse) to perform its function as an employers' union and these lay down the general lines for wage negotiations. The practical conduct of negotiations is first planned by the individual departmental bodies.

Negotiations are only held at top level between the Trade Union Federation and the Federal Chamber of Trade and Industry if a decision on working conditions in general (such as shorter working hours) is to be taken. Otherwise it is the subordinate regional and departmental branches of the Trade Unions and the Chambers which negotiate. The agreements concluded have a relatively wide coverage; of the collective agreements concluded in 1968, 190 had nation-wide coverage, 396 were Land collective agreements and only 16 were works agreements (these proportions also hold good for the longer term). The individual Trade Unions have traditionally different negotiating policies which have only little changed in the last decade. While the food-stuff workers negotiate in small groups and try to control the development of earnings, the Metal Workers Union wants a comprehensive wage agreement for all its members and tolerates wage drift.

The centralization of collective agreements in large sectors of the economy is a source of wage drift, which has become stronger with the drying up of the labour supply. Wage drift in Austria is only partly caused by individual wage increases; it is often the result of plant agreements between management and works council, which take account of the particular economic conditions governing the enterprise. Increases in wage rates at branch level which tend to be relatively lower are often followed by negotiations at plant level. Moreover, earnings sometimes change at plant level between rounds of negotiations, in which case wage increases at plant level are sometimes only granted as an advance on account of increases to be agreed in subsequent collective negotiations.

The Trade Unions have tried to regain control over effective earnings by including earnings clauses in collective agreements. In some branches (iron and metal industry, chemical industry, paper and woodworking industry, footwear industry) wage agreements, in addition to raising minimum wage rates, regularly provide for rises in effective earnings, although the percentage rise in them is as a rule considerably smaller than the rise in wage rates.

The duration of agreements varies widely, but there is now more uniformity than in the 50's and less sensitivity to booms and slumps. In the past decade there were new rounds of wage negotiations about every one-and-a-half years, but this rhythm did not apply to all sectors of the economy. In commerce and the building trades annual wage increases are the rule, because the Trade Unions prefer to negotiate before the Christmas season or the beginning of the building season, while in the services sector agreements run for very long periods (about three years in the hairdressing trade). As, however, the largest categories of workers (iron and metal industries, salary earners in industry and trade, chemical and textile industries and most branches of the foodstuffs industry) start their wage negotiations at about the same time every one-and-a-half years, it seems quite right to speak of rounds of wage negotiations in Austria.

The negotiating partners usually manage to reach agreement without labour strife, and friction is only serious towards the end of a boom, when prices are still rising steeply despite falling growth rates (1956, 1961-1962, 1965-1966). Strikes reached an all time low in 1971, when only 29,614 working hours were lost through strikes and lock-outs involving 2,431 workers (the corresponding figures for 1970 were 212,928 and 7,547).

Collective agreements are not usually renewed in their entirety; instead supplementary agreements are made altering certain clauses only. Wage rates are at the heart of the negotiations. The trade unions have gradually succeeded in increasing fringe benefits and the claim to

13

a 13th and 14th month's wage is now generally accepted, the money being paid in the form of special allowances (holiday pay and Christmas bonus). For long there was little interest in improvements in working conditions which did not involve pay rises. Certain sectors led the way in shortening working hours and this trend was sanctioned in an umbrella collective agreement as from 1970 (whereby hours per week are to be reduced from 45 to 40 by 1975 in three stages). Only in recent years have demands been put forward for contractual protection against rationalisation risks and for improved training facilities (training leave), and just lately discussion of industrial co-determination and profit-sharing has started.

Wage rates are normally increased by means of a uniform percentage addition, but here and there a levelling effect is sought by raising wage rates by the same absolute amount or by raising the lowest grades (women and unskilled labour) most. A similar effect is produced by real earnings clauses in collective agreements which raise actual wages less than minimum wages, but these refinements are not enough to be able to alter wage structures decisively, especially as wage drift tends to counteract them. Wage indexation is the exception in Austria, although in the paper industry and the public service there are long-term wage agreements linked to the consumer price index.

So far the Government has avoided interfering directly with wage structure (apart from the immediate post-war period). It has respected the autonomy of the authorized negotiating bodies and has exerted its influence mainly through the joint institutions to be discussed later.

PRICE FORMATION

The Government has always had wide powers to control prices, but it no longer makes full use of them, partly because economic conditions have improved, partly because the success of price regulation is doubtful in some cases. At present about a quarter of the goods (including rent and local rates) in the consumer price index shopping basket come under official price control.

Under the Price Control Law the Ministry of the Interior, in agreement with other Ministries concerned and after hearing the views of the Price Commission (on which the Federal Chamber of Trade and Industry, the Presidents' Conference of the Land Chambers of Trade and Industry and the Chambers of Labour Conference are represented, as well as various Ministries*), can fix "economically justifiable" maximum prices

* Federal Ministries of Trade and Industry, Agriculture and Forestry, Social Affairs, Finance and Transport.

for the commodities listed in the Annex to the Law. At present the retail prices of most staple foodstuffs (flour, bread, milk, butter, some
kinds of cheese and sugar), liquid fuels, electricity and certain pharma-
ceuticals are officially controlled, as are also producer prices for milk
and cereals which are subsidized under the agricultural market regulations (other farm prices are affected by market regulations and restrictions on foreign trade). The power to fix maximum prices is not at
present used in respect of a number of foodstuffs, solid fuels and raw
materials. Applications to raise controlled prices or have an official
price fixed for a new product which is subject to price regulation have
to be submitted to the competent Ministry, which screens them and then
passes them to the Price Commission for an opinion. Decisions are
either notified individually or in a public announcement by the Ministry
of the Interior. Apart from that, Article 3a of the Price Control Law
empowers the Minister of the Interior to fix prices for a maximum period of six months, if the three Chambers belonging to the Price Commission and the Trade Union Federation state unanimously that prices are
being raised in an entire sector of the economy or by an enterprise
which dominates the market.

Under existing trade regulations the Land Authorities can fix maximum prices for retail articles of first necessity and for certain services.
Government rent control on older residential buildings has recently been
relaxed somewhat (prices are de-controlled for new leases).

The Government has a further price control instrument in the Anti-
Profiteering Law, which prohibits charging appreciably more than the
normal prices at the place of sale for commodities constituting necessities of life. Decisions on whether there is overcharging lie with the
administrative authorities or with the law courts.

In recent years increasing use has been made of authority under the
Cartel Law to promote price competition by rejecting, at the request
of one of the three Chambers, price recommendations in cases where
existing prices to the end consumer lie considerably below the recom-
mended prices in an important segment of total turnover (Net Price
Regulations). Lately, moreover, the Government has also helped to
keep prices down by periodically making selective cuts in import duties.

For a long time certain branches of nationalized industry (the iron
industry and coal mining) pursued a policy of low prices which enabled
the other sectors of the economy to obtain cheap raw materials, but the
merits of the policy became doubtful when the low domestic prices were
no longer compensated by favourable export prices and in recent years
it has been given up. The important government sector of the economy
helps to keep prices down and make price control effective by requiring
its suppliers to have their prices approved by the voluntary price control
boards (Joint Price and Wage Commission).

THE JOINT PRICE AND WAGE COMMISSION

Background

The Joint Price and Wage Commission grew out of the "Economic Commission" of the post-war period. While the latter's activities ("Prices and Wages Agreements") could not prevent post-war inflation, they were important in laying the groundwork for the institutionalized co-operation between organised economic interests and the Government which characterizes Austrian economic policy.

The inflationary trend continued after the last Prices and Wages Agreement in the middle of 1951 and in the autumn of that year the Federal Chamber of Trade and Industry and the Federation of Austrian Industry appealed to their members to reduce prices where possible, while the Trade Union Federation announced that it would accept a wage freeze. Prices did in fact fall in the following months and the success of this stabilization policy was consolidated by a business recession and a restrictive monetary and fiscal policy.

After the 1952 stabilization crisis prices rose only slightly, so that in the following years there was little activity in the field of incomes policy and it was not until 1956 that boom conditions again drove prices up steeply. This development brought the "Economic Commission" back into action again and eventually led to the formation of the Joint Commission on the lines proposed earlier by the Trade Union Federation. The formal initiative for setting up this institution was a resolution of the Ministerial Council urging the main employers' and workers' organisations to make arrangements to keep prices down; price and wage increases were to be scrutinized by a Commission. Nevertheless, the initiatives for institutionalizing prices and incomes policy in Austria came from the employers' and workers' organisations.

Composition and Functions

The Joint Commission was set up in March, 1957, under the above-mentioned resolution of the Ministerial Council. It is composed of four Government representatives (Federal Chancellor, Minister of the Interior, Minister of Trade and Industry and Minister of Social Affairs) and of two representatives each from the three main Chambers (Federal Chamber of Trade and Industry, Chamber of Agriculture and Chamber of Labour) and from the Trade Union Federation (in practice the meetings are usually attended by more representatives from the non-Government bodies). This structure ensured equal representation of employers and workers (hence the Trade Union Federation's membership of the Commission in addition to that of the Chamber of Labour, whereas there were no representatives from the Federation of Austrian Industry on the other side) and also, until the end of the "grand coalition" in 1966, equal representation of the two major political parties (hitherto the Federal Chancellor and the Minister of Trade and Industry had belonged to one of them and the Ministers of the Interior and Social Affairs to the other). However, this factor is of no vital importance, since the decisions of the Joint Commission have to be unanimous.

The Joint Commission meets once a month. Before the meetings Presidents of the non-Government bodies, with their Secretaries-General and Economic Advisers, meet to discuss the agenda. These "President's discussions" have acquired increasing importance, especially since the end of the "grand coalition"; they enable potential causes of strife to be removed in advance and they are also increasingly assuming the functions of a supreme arbitration board. The Federal Chancellor or the Minister of the Interior takes the chair at meetings of the Joint Commission itself and the Office of the Federal Chancellor keeps the minutes of the meetings, as the Commission has no secretariat of its own. Since 1968 there has been a so-called exchange of views on economic policy every three months (after the revised economic forecasts have come out), at which the Head of the Economic Research Institute, the President of the National Bank and the Minister of Finance report on the economic situation.

The Joint Commission works on a voluntary basis and represents employers' and workers' organisations jointly with the Government; it has no legal authority nor means of applying direct sanctions. Only the Government could impose sanctions (as it threatened to do when the Commission was set up), but in practice it has hardly ever done so. The Joint Commission was set up to control price and wage trends and this is still its main activity, so that it is a typical instrument of incomes policy (although not designed as such). In addition, however, thanks to the tripartite structure it has become an instrument which gives the employers' and workers' organisations a voice in government economic policy in general and conversely enables the Government to make sure of co-operation from these organisations in its economic policy measures.

The Joint Commission was not set up in its present form, but is the result of continuous development. The prevailing economic situation strongly influenced the forms it has taken, as well as its original conception. Following a period of calm in the 1958-1959 recession, the prices and wages spiral began again with the boom at the beginning of the 60s. This led to criticism of the ineffectiveness of the Joint Commission and eventually, in 1962, to an agreement between the

Federal Chamber of Trade and Industry and the Trade Union Federation (the Raab-Olah Agreement) establishing a second Sub-Committee of the Commission to deal with wage questions, in addition to the original Sub-Committee for price questions, and modifying the price control procedure. At the end of 1963 a third Sub-Committee, the Economic and Social Advisory Board, was set up (the Raab-Benya Agreement). This extension of the Joint Commission was a further step from price-wage-control to economic co-determination of the interest groups. It was especially important for the labour organisations, because it enabled them not only to influence prices but also the whole range of economic activities.

The Wages Sub-Committee

The Wages Sub-Committee was set up in order to reduce the work load on the Joint Commission, which had originally itself controlled wages. Its members include only representatives of workers and employers (two each from the Federal Chamber of Trade and Industry and the Trade Union Federation, whose subordinate bodies usually conduct the wage negotiations, and one each from the Chamber of Labour and the Chamber of Agriculture). It meets every fortnight under the alternate chairmanship of the Trade Union Federation and the Federal Chamber of Trade and Industry. Decisions have to be unanimous. If a question cannot be decided within six weeks, it is referred to the Joint Commission, which has a further five weeks to decide it, failing which an application awaiting decision is held to have been granted (although the Raab-Benya Agreement stated that decisions should be reached before the expiry of the time limit).

The Joint Commission exercises its control over wages as follows. A particular trade union informs the Trade Union Federation of its intention to start wage negotiations and the Federation applies to the Wages Sub-Committee for its agreement. The fact that applications are submitted to the Joint Commission through the Trade Union Federation means that they have been co-ordinated in advance in the trade union machinery. Indeed, the trade union headquarters have a voice in fixing the date and sequence and in some degree the extent of individual wage claims. There also exists a Working Party on Wages Policy for internal co-ordination which deals not only with wage demands, but also attempts to set and realize common objectives of wage policy. The Wages Sub-Committee can authorize the start of negotiations forthwith, but it usually asks for preliminary talks to be held between two representatives each from the employers and workers and for a report on their outcome. It can also hold over an application or refuse it outright (but rarely does so). Lastly, it can refer the application to the Joint Commission, and it must do this if unanimity cannot be reached, or the application involves a matter of principal, or is likely to lead to an application for a price increase. The outcome of the wage negotiations has to be submitted to the Wages Sub-Committee for approval and at this stage the same procedural paths are open as in authorizing the start of negotiations, but they are seldom made use of in practice. Although the Joint Commission cannot directly influence the content of wage agreements, it has in its brief an arsenal of instruments for postponing them. It was informally agreed in the Presidents' discussions that the duration of collective agreements should not normally be less than 16 months.

The Prices Sub-Committee

The Prices Sub-Committee is composed of six members, one each from the four main employers' and workers' organisations and from the Ministries of the Interior and Finance. It meets once a week under the chairmanship of the Federal Chamber of Trade and Industry, which also provides the Secretariat. Applications by individual firms or branches for price increases, if approved by the Ministry of the Interior and the Chamber of Labour as ready for examination by the Sub-Committee, are sent in by the Federal Chamber of Trade and Industry; if not approved, the applicants are asked to provide further justification. The Prices Sub-Committee can accept an application unanimously (in its entirety or in part), hold it over, or refer it to the Joint Commission. Since 1962 the time limit for dealing with applications has been the same as for the Wages Sub-Committee (including the proviso that decisions should be reached before the expiry of the time limit).

Originally the Prices Sub-Committee's terms of reference covered all commodities and it dealt with some 200 standard articles which were held to show typical price trends. Its coverage is widest in the case of price increases in industry (of which it covered some 60% initially), while in other sectors the Joint Commission has less say. In the services sector price control has always been limited to a few key items (e. g. hairdressing and cinemas). The Prices Sub-Committee's coverage was gradually reduced (partly for practical reasons) and today the following items are free from control by the Joint Commission: officially regulated prices and tariffs, import prices, fees charged by professional groups which do not belong to the Federal Chamber of Trade and Industry, seasonal price variations (fruit, vegetables, meat), most service charges and fashion goods prices (clothing, footwear, etc.). Price variations are also normally excluded if they leave the trading margin unaltered when a price increase has already been approved for an earlier stage in the distribution chain. Unlike official price controls, the Joint Commission also excludes new products and their profit margins. Thus the Commission's controls are in practice confined to proprietary goods, staple commodities and standard services. The number of applications handled per year varies (according to the state of business) from 150 to 350, of which from 20 to 40 relate to services. The proportion of articles in the consumer price index shopping basket subject to the Joint Commission's price control, either fully or in part, is at present something under one-fifth (in the early 60s it was still almost one-quarter, the decrease being partly due to changes in the pattern of expenditure). The proportion of consumer goods whose prices are controlled (including government control) has dropped below 50% and, while the percentage may be higher for raw materials and investment goods controlled by the Joint Commission, here also it is declining.

When the Joint Commission was first set up, the Prices Sub-Committee was given the directive that price increases were only justified if substantial changes in costs had occurred which could not be offset by rationalization measures and increased productivity. Accordingly applicants have to satisfy the Prices Sub-Committee that their costs have gone up. This they usually do by means of a rough calculation under three headings showing the changes in expenditure on staff, materials, and other items and the weighting (share in total costs) given to each heading. Employers have so far refused to submit detailed figures and they do not usually state in their applications the degree of plant utilization and increase in productivity in their enterprises or the market situation. The only allowance made for these factors is that sometimes the price increase authorized is reduced by a percentage based on a rough estimate. When applications are made by whole branches of industry, the Prices Sub-Committee is usually given statements of the costs in a few representative concerns to base its decisions on.

In 1962 price control was strengthened and extended by the Raab-Olah Agreement, under which firms which raise their prices by more than the approved amount or without authorization are summoned to submit an application to the Prices Sub-Committee within 14 days. It also provides in theory for imposing sanctions; under Article 3a of the Price Control Law the Minister of the Interior can, in the case of an enterprise which dominates the market, fix an official price for six months, but only if all four of the central employers' and workers' organisations request him to do so, a condition which has not yet been fulfilled. At the end of 1971 the powers to impose sanctions were widened by an agreement between employers and workers and Article 3a of the Price Control Law was made applicable also to enterprises which do not dominate the market. In addition the Chamber of Trade and Industry and the Chamber of Agriculture undertook to approve an application to the Ministry of the Interior for price control in cases where an enterprise which dominates an industry or market does not apply to the Joint Commission within three weeks after being requested to do so by the Chamber of Trade and Industry.

The Joint Commission now has a further Committee for dealing with price questions. When the German Mark was revalued the Government, in agreement with the Joint Commission, lowered the import duties on a number of products in order to counteract the expected price increases, whereupon a Special Committee was appointed (for a limited period) with the same membership as the Prices Sub-Committee to see that the reduction in duties was passed on to the end consumer.

The Economic and Social Advisory Board

At the end of 1963 the Economic and Social Advisory Board was set up and was the third and last permanent sub-committee of the Joint Commission. It reflects the logical extension of the Joint Commission's activities, which had hitherto been confined mainly to wages and prices policy, to economic policy as a whole. Its creation was partly due to the growing conviction that a broader scientific basis was required for economic policy measures designed to solve the structural problems evident in the falling growth rates and rising inflation of the first half of the 60s. In its practical manifestation the Advisory Board, like the Joint Commission, was a compromise. While it did not come up to expectations as an aid to economic programming, it extended workers' co-determination above plant level.

The Economic and Social Advisory Board was given the task of studying economic and social policy questions in the context of the economy as a whole, and its findings are to serve as a basis for recommendations to be made by the Joint Commission to the Federal Government. The Advisory Board differs from similar institutions abroad by being both a group of expert advisers and a body for resolving conflicts of interest. It is composed of three advisers from each of the four main employers' and workers' organisations and of two secretaries-general (provided by the Chambers of Labour Conference and the Federal Chamber of Trade and Industry), the Chairmanship rotating twice a year among the four organisations. Its pattern of membership ensures that in the pursuit of its expert investigations it tries to reconcile differences between the bodies concerned (minority votes are possible, but rare). While this function makes the Advisory Board's work more difficult, it brings the advantage that the Board's recommendations are such as can be carried out, and they are indeed carried out by the Government to a great extent (but it undoubtedly has drawbacks also, e.g. it prevents some alternatives from ever being discussed in public). For its practical work the Advisory Board has set up permanent or ad hoc Working

Parties comprising numerous advisers from government departments, research centres, higher education centres, employers' and workers' organisations and business enterprises. The Economic and Social Advisory Board's reports and recommendations are sent to the Presidents of the four main employers' and workers' organisations and, if approved by them, are then forwarded through the Joint Commission to the Government.

Part II

THE AUSTRIAN ECONOMY IN THE SIXTIES

by

Dr. Hannes Suppanz

AIMS OF THE PRICES AND INCOMES POLICY

The declared aims of Austrian economic policy in general and of the prices and incomes policy in particular were essentially the same as in other OECD countries, namely, internal and external monetary stability with a high level of employment, a satisfactory growth rate, and a fair distribution of incomes. The success of a country's prices and incomes policy is to be judged, not only by the extent to which these partly contradictory aims are attained, but also by whether violent cyclical swings have been avoided and industrial peace preserved.

In Austria, as in other countries, incomes policy priorities have changed in the course of time and naturally the different parties responsible for incomes policy (the employers' and workers' organisations and the Government) have always stressed different themes. For years price stability was the main theme, which is not surprising, as Austrian incomes policy began during the battle against post-war inflation waged jointly by both sides of industry and the Government. The Joint Commission also was at first regarded only as an instrument for controlling prices and wages, and the first years of its life were marked by periodic stabilization programmes and price and wage freezes. Even today Austrian economic policy does not claim to include an incomes policy as understood abroad (it lays down no official quantitative guidelines for trends in incomes and does not control incomes other than wages), but only claims to have a policy for wages and prices. Nevertheless, the policy has gradually been changing. Whereas at first it consisted merely in a series of short-term ad hoc stabilization measures, it later

23

became an instrument of counter-cyclical policy, ranking with all the other instruments of economic policy. The Trade Unions made counter-cyclical wages policy their official slogan, and prices policy also became increasingly dominated by the question of the correct timing of counter-cyclical policy, after having earlier been preoccupied by cost criteria. Since the Economic and Social Advisory Board was set up, the growth aspects of incomes policy have increasingly captured attention. By giving up their aggressive wages policy and observing industrial peace the workers considered that they were helping to remedy the structural weaknesses which appeared in the Austrian economy in the first half of the 60s and to maintain Austria's competitive strength in world markets.

Compared with monetary stability and economic growth, incomes distribution policy took lower priority. Unlike many other countries, no attempt was made in Austria to impose a redistribution of incomes and anyhow such action would probably have been inconsistent with the nature of an Austrian prices and incomes policy formulated voluntarily by both sides of industry. The trade union "solidaristic wages policy" strategy, which aims at raising the lowest wage rates most in collective agreements, was helped by the Joint Commission, since the latter enabled the Trade Union Federation to co-ordinate wage negotiations, but against this was the disadvantage of a highly centralized wages policy imparting a momentum to the structure of wages which gave rise to the phenomenon of wage drift.

DEVELOPMENTS FROM 1960 TO 1970
AND THE INTERNATIONAL BACKGROUND

The following description of the Austrian economy in the 60s should suffice for assessing the results of Austria's prices and incomes policy. The present-day incomes policy institutions were in fact set up as early as 1957, but owing to the recession in the following years they were not put to the test until the early 60s. The attached Tables give figures for the most important target magnitudes in incomes policy, namely economic growth, employment, prices, costs and wages, the balance of payments and industrial peace. Developments in Austria are shown alongside those in comparable small European industrial countries (Belgium, the Netherlands, Sweden and Switzerland) and in the main trading partners (the Federal Republic of Germany, Italy and Great Britain) and also, where data are available, alongside developments in the EEC, the EFTA and the European OECD countries as a whole.

The Austrian economy did not expand in the 60s as fast as in the previous decade, but the average annual growth rate of the GNP (4.7%) was almost as high as in the Federal Republic of Germany and the average for the European OECD countries (Table 1). Contrary to the trend in most other industrial countries, the rate of growth accelerated from the first to the second half of the decade (from 4.4% to 5.1% per year). This reflected temporary structural weaknesses in the Austrian economy; in the first half of the 60s the progressive integration of the EEC economies and the falling demand for raw materials led to a downturn in the export growth rate, stagnation in industrial investment and under-utilization of capacity, but in recent years these difficulties have been overcome by diversifying exports more and improving the industrial structure. The Austrian situation is seen in a more favourable light by taking per capita figures; in the 60s real GNP per inhabitant rose appreciably faster in Austria (4.1% per year) than in neighbouring Germany (3.6%) and Switzerland (2.9%), while of the other countries shown only Belgium (marginally) and Italy had higher growth rates.

In the 60s economic growth was achieved entirely by raising productivity; real GNP per gainfully employed person rose by 5.0% per year, which was faster than in all the other countries shown except Italy. The improvement in the economic situation in the second half of the decade is clear from the rise in overall economic productivity which shot up from 4.4% (1960/1965) to 5.7% (1965/1970), while the trend in industrial productivity showed an even steeper increase (from 4.0% to 6.3%). The rapid industrial expansion in the late 60s drove the share of the tertiary sector in the real GNP down below its 1960 level and raised the share of the secondary sector to over 50% (Table 10).

In comparison with other countries Austria shows up well, not only in its rate of growth, but also in the steadiness of its growth (Table 7). According to an OECD investigation*, the level of demand from 1955 to 1970 varied less in Austria than in any of the other countries shown (as measured by deviations of real GNP from the average trend), a result which is the more remarkable as cyclical swings in Austria followed the same trend as in the Federal Republic of Germany and the European OECD countries as a whole (although with a slight time lag; in 1966 there was a delayed investment boom in Austria and in 1970 the rate of growth rose, unlike in other countries). The relative mild fluctuations of the growth rate were, of course, also a consequence of the fact that, due to the difficulties mentioned above, the growth potential could not be fully utilized in the mid 60s. The intensity of the fluctuations was about the same in both cycles of the 60s. As the agricultural sector accounts for a fairly large proportion of the GNP, compared with other countries, figures have also been worked out for the

* Austria, "OECD Economic Surveys", August, 1971.

fluctuations in the GNP leaving out agriculture and forestry and they show wider fluctuations in demand in the second half of the 60s than in the first half, although considerably less so than in the Federal Republic of Germany. This means that Austria, being a small country, was not able to escape external economic influences entirely, but managed to keep them within bounds. This impression is further strengthened by the most recent developments. In the middle of 1972, i.e. two years after the boom in European industrial countries began to subside, the boom in Austria, which had started in 1967, was still continuing. This unusually prolonged boom, accompanied by relative stability, was partly due to a well-timed succession of demand streams (at first it was supported mainly by demand from abroad and the upswing in domestic investment and consumption only began in 1970), but it was also made possible by the circumstance that capacity had never been fully stretched in the preceding boom in the mid-sixties.

In the 60s the number of gainfully employed persons in Austria fell slightly. The number of persons in dependent employment increased faster in the first half of the decade and after that only slightly, mainly due to the exodus of self-employed persons from agriculture (the percentage of persons engaged in agriculture dropped from 24 to 17, see Table 10) and in recent years also to the increasing employment of foreigners (1971, about 6% of the labour force).

Since the beginning of the 60s there has been full employment in Austria and manpower reserves are almost exhausted (the 48% gainfully employed quota is high compared with other countries). The strain on the labour market is not truly reflected in the unemployment rate (Table 2 and Table 7), which is likely to be inflated compared with other countries, since many of the registered unemployed in Austria are not readily employable. As regards trends in unemployment, it is noticeable that Austria is the only country in the Table with a rate of unemployment which fell in the second half of the 60s. Yet the 1967/1968 slump hit the labour market harder than the 1962/1963 slump. Employment decreased in absolute terms and the ratio of unemployed to vacancies rose higher than in the first half of the 60s, but in spite of this the strain on the labour market had reached a new high by 1970.

Austria is a country with relatively little labour strife. While it does not have such an exceptional record as, for example, Switzerland (Table 6), losses from strikes are considerably lower than in countries like Great Britain or Italy. Industrial peace can be compared to what it is in Sweden, the Netherlands, Belgium and Germany. Taking the 60s as a whole, Austria performed even better than these countries (if one takes account of its size) as regards the numbers of workers involved in labour disputes, and the duration of labour disputes was certainly shorter in Austria than in all the other countries shown. Moreover, the picture is somewhat distorted by taking averages for so many years, because the last major strikes in Austria took place in 1965/1966, since when industrial peace has largely prevailed, whereas labour disputes increased in other countries.

In the 60s the rise in prices was less in Austria than the average for the European OECD countries (Table 3 and Table 8). The rate of inflation, as calculated by the GNP deflator, was 3.7% (OECD in Europe 4.1%) and so was only higher than in the Federal Republic of Germany (3.5%) and Belgium (3.3%). The drop in the rate of growth in the first half of the 60s was accompanied by a steeper rise in prices (4.1% per year in 1960/1965), but in the second half the rise slowed down again to near the trend in the 50s (1965/1970, 3.3%) and was the least for all the countries shown. This was a result of under-utilization of capacity at the start of the upswing, the delayed expansion of domestic demand and not least the restraint shown by the Trade Unions in their wages policy. In 1970/1971, when domestic demand expanded and the situation in labour markets and commodity markets became tighter, prices in Austria rose faster, but not as fast as the international average.

A comparison of consumer prices gives a similar picture. The annual increase of 3.6% was rather below the average for the OECD in Europe (3.8%), but was more than in Germany, Belgium and Switzerland, while in the second half of the 60s prices also rose less in Italy. The drop in the rate of price increases from the first to the second half of the decade (unlike the GNP deflator) was entirely due to the sudden rise in the prices of seasonal agricultural products in 1965; if they are left out, the trend of consumer prices is found to have been fairly steady throughout the 60s and only slightly below the trend of the GNP deflator.

During the 50s consumer prices had risen noticeably less than the general price level. One of the reasons for the subsequent steeper rise in prices was the development of officially regulated prices. From 1961 to 1967 officially regulated prices (staple foodstuffs and scales of charges), which had been kept steady for years, suffered several sharp increases and as some of these occurred at unfavourable moments in business cycles and at seasonal peaks, various secondary price movements were triggered off (spreading of cost increases and wage claims). In recent years officially controlled prices have again helped to keep down the level of consumer prices, because they were raised by less than average amounts and more gradually, but meanwhile imported inflationary forces have strengthened. Just lately, despite the continuation of the cyclical rise in prices, it became necessary to raise a number of officially controlled prices which the authorities had long delayed raising for counter-cyclical policy reasons.

Labour costs per unit of production followed a similar trend to that of prices. In the economy as a whole their rate of increase dropped from 5.1% in the first half of the 60s to 3.1% in the second half, while in the industrial sector it dropped from 3.7% to 1.9%. The lower rate of increase was the result of lower wage increases and a steeper rise in productivity. In the second half of the 60s the rise in industrial labour costs was less than in any other country shown and, taking the average for the decade, it was only in Belgium that labour costs rose more slowly. If changes in the values of currencies are allowed for, labour costs in Great Britain are seen to have increased less than in Austria, while they rose distinctly faster in the Federal Republic of Germany. Thus, as regards labour costs, Austria's competitive position abroad improved markedly in the second half of the 60s after marking time in the first half.

In Austria wages rose at the average rate for the other countries (Table 4). Hourly earnings in manufacturing industry rose by 8.6% per year, or at about the same rate as in the Federal Republic of Germany and Sweden, but faster than in Belgium, Great Britain and Switzerland. From the first to the second half of the 60s the rise in effective earnings declined from 9.2% to 8%, but against that the rise in standard rates increased somewhat (from 6.5% in 1960/1965 to 7.2% in 1965/1970). However, Austria's 6.9% average increase in standard wage rates during the 60s gives the country here also an intermediate position among the other countries shown. Compared with other countries, wage drift was high (only in Sweden was it higher in relation to official policy wage rates), but it decreased considerably from the first to the second half of the 60s (from 2.7% to 0.8% per year), as it did in most countries.*

The reduced wage drift reflected both the easier position on the labour market in 1967/1968 and the counter-cyclical wages policy of the Trade Unions. The so-called counter-cyclical wages policy which the Trade Unions have been following in recent years is in fact a rather less pro-cyclical wages policy reflecting the intention of the Trade Unions not to let the rate of wage increases drop below a certain minimum level in times of recession, but in return not to exploit fully the advantage which a tight labour market gives them when negotiating wage rates in boom conditions. In other words it narrows the gap between upper and lower rates of wage increase. The wage freeze under the

---

* In Austria effective earnings consist of hourly earnings excluding special allowances, but including overtime earnings. The standard rates are the minimum wages per hour worked. Wage drift is calculated as the difference between the rates of change in earnings and in standard rates. It is true that for some years the figures for earnings in Austria are distorted by the fact that they could not be insulated from the effects of overtime, as a comparison with other wage surveys shows, but this does not affect the long-term trend of earnings and wage drift.

stabilization agreement at the beginning of the sixties led to a sharp increase in wage drift (Table 9), but in the slump in the mid-sixties the Trade Unions succeeded in raising wage rates, although only slightly, so that in 1968 wage drift was actually negative. The annual rates of increase concerning also normal hours shown in the Table were much influenced by the shortening of working time and the timing of wage rounds. Thus in 1970 over four percentage points in the rate of increase were due to shorter normal working hours for the same weekly wages, while the high rates reached in 1965 and 1971 were due to the wage rounds held in January in those years. When separate collective agreements are considered, it will be found that the increases in standard rates agreed since 1968 have indeed steepened from one round to the next in tune with boom conditions, but that they have not as yet exceeded 1965/1966 rates of increase despite the unusually tight situation in the labour market. However, the Trade Unions have had to face an increased wage drift and organisational problems as a result of pursuing this wages policy, which is intended to smooth out trade cycles and, while it was at first aimed also at helping to overcome structural weaknesses in the Austrian economy by promoting an investment boom, it may more recently have also been motivated by consideration for the one-party Socialist Government. Nevertheless, it has so far proved possible to master these problems (unlike in the Federal Republic of Germany, there have so far only been occasional wild-cat strikes). Austria is one of the few countries where the trend which wages have actually followed could always be explained by wage functions and the credit for their sober behaviour should no doubt be given to Austria's incomes policy.

In the short term the balance of payments followed the opposite trend to economic growth, but for the 60s as a whole it was favourable. Currency reserves rose by about $ 1,000 million during the decade and so more than doubled, but this result was only achieved thanks to massive capital imports and corresponding foreign indebtedness. Over the whole of the period under study the invisible balance was slightly unfavourable, but the deficit can be explained by statistical discrepancies. Receipts from tourism normally sufficed to cover the trade deficit and it was only in the mid-60s, when the deficit tended to widen owing to the progressive integration of the EEC economies and the structural weaknesses in industry, and when receipts from foreign tourists were depressed by the recession in the Federal Republic of Germany, that the invisible balance moved further into the red. The situation has definitely improved since 1967; the lost market share has been regained thanks to the more favorable structure of exports and the slow rise in labour costs and the surplus on the invisible balance has increased considerably. The soundness of the balance of payments may be seen from the ratio of currency reserves to imports, which remained steady at about 50% during the 60s and in 1970 was exceeded only by Switzerland, although in the Federal Republic of Germany the ratio was almost as high as in Austria (Table 5).

INCOME DISTRIBUTION AND WAGE STRUCTURE

In the 60s there was a noticeable shift in the distribution of the national income in favour of wage incomes. This took place at the expense of farm incomes, while the share of other incomes from property and entrepreneurship remained practically constant (Table 11). The share of wages rose from 59% in 1960 to 66.5% in 1968 and then dropped to 64.2% in 1970 (Table 9). It rose from 61.1% to 64.9% from the first to the second half of the 60s, which was less than the average for the European OECD countries. An analysis of the incidence of taxation and social insurance contributions on wage incomes and non-wage incomes shows that the re-distribution effects have hardly varied in the long term. Quite recently, however, the picture has changed. In the past the above-average incidence of taxation on wages had always been offset by tax reforms, but since 1968 the situation has sharply deteriorated to the detriment of wage incomes and it is doubtful whether the tax reforms planned for 1973 will be sufficient to correct this trend.

The increase in the share of the national income taken by wages was in the long term entirely due to the structural change in the working population brought about by transfers from independent employment (particularly in agriculture) to dependent employment. If this structural change is ignored, the long-term share of wages is found not to have changed. Taking the occupational structure in 1960 as a basis, the share of wages in 1970 works out at 1% larger (Table 9), while its increase from the first to the second half of the decade dropped to about 2%. If the 50s are included in the comparison, it is seen that this increase in the share of wages did no more than recover the ground lost between 1954 and 1960. An enquiry by the Chamber of Labour has shown that over the past half century the distribution of incomes in Austria as between wages and other earnings has remained constant. The further increase in the share of wages in the 1967/68 slump and its sharp decline in the 1968/70 boom reflects the counter cyclical wages policy of the Trade Unions. Since then the share of the national income taken by wages has again been increasing, but it is unlikely to regain its 1968 level before 1972, and if structural changes in the working population are excluded, it will not reach its 1968 level even in 1972.

In the absence of adequate statistical data further analysis has to be confined to piecemeal information on the structure of wages. International comparative figures for the taxation of wages show that the degree of bunching in the levels of wage incomes in Austria is quite low (only in Great Britain is it lower) and hardly varies in the long term. The levelling effect of income tax weakens as incomes rise, which is why proposals to make income tax rates rise less steeply have regularly been a subject of negotiation between the Minister of Finance and the

Trade Unions and have been incorporated in the blueprint for a comprehensive incomes policy. The last two examples of this were the tax reforms at the end of 1967 as part of the "Big Bargain" (which will be dealt with later) and the advancing of the date for the reductions in income tax from 1973 to the middle of 1972. In the spring of 1972 the Trade Unions stated that the extent of their wage demands in the forthcoming wage round would depend on whether the Finance Minister brought forward the tax reforms he had announced for 1973. After protracted negotiations between employers, workers and the Finance Minister, which included a detailed discussion of the whole tax reform scheme, it was finally agreed not to bring forward the tax reforms, but to reduce the tax liability of all persons paying income tax by a fixed amount as from the middle of 1972.

An analysis of wage structure in industry and trade shows that the levelling up which had started at the beginning of the 50s continued during the past 10 years, although at a slower rate. The post-war prices and wages agreements had favoured the lower wage categories (women and unskilled workers) and in many cases these categories were given better-than-average treatment in subsequent years also, although the trend lacked uniformity and varied from one period to another. These efforts of the Trade Unions to establish a solidaristic wages policy are also visible, although less clearly, in the trend of effective earnings; in the 60s female workers bettered their position vis-à-vis male workers, as did wage earners vis-à-vis salary earners. The rise in piece rates in the 60s was below average in all categories and the ratio of piece-rate wages to time-rate wages and bonus-system wages declined.

When compared with other countries, wages in the different branches of industry diverged rather widely, and this is true both of earnings and of wage rates, as the Austrian scale of standard rates comprises many sub-divisions. However, international comparisons are of doubtful value owing to the different systems of classifying the branches. Though there were only minor differences between the rates of change of wages the diversity of effective earnings, but also of wage rates, widened steadily during the 60s and wage drift again increased, especially in recent times, due to the pull of economic conditions. Wage payments above standard rates reached an all-time high, accounting for about 30% of industrial workers' earnings and about 25% of industrial employees' earnings. They were strongly influenced by the extent to which wage negotiations were centralized; thus they accounted for only 7% of earnings in the foodstuffs industry, but for over 50% in ironworks.

To sum up, it may be said that in the 60s the Austrian economy, despite temporary difficulties in the first half of the decade, developed very favourably as compared with other countries. The rises in prices and costs were less than abroad, economic growth was as fast, the rise in productivity was above average, the level of employment remained high, industrial peace was for the most part preserved, and the balance of payments was not endangered. Although Austria is heavily dependent on foreign trade (which accounts for more than a quarter of the GNP), cyclical swings in the economy were kept within narrower limits than abroad. The difficulties in assessing the success of economic policy measures are well known and the inter-dependence of so many factors makes any deduction open to question, but it seems possible nevertheless, on the basis of the available figures, to venture some conclusions regarding the influence of prices and incomes policy in Austria on economic developments.

Even allowing for the fact that the economic situation was undoubtedly more difficult in the first half of the sixties than in the second half, the economic history of the sixties leaves one with the impression that the flexibility, and consequently the effectiveness, of incomes policy has increased as a result of the lessons which the institutions concerned have been constantly learning. At the beginning of the decade, full employment was reached, but at the same time the rise in productivity slowed down owing to the structural problems already mentioned and the struggle over the distribution of incomes grew fiercer. By the middle of the decade the structural difficulties had been overcome, productivity was rising again more steeply and a new upswing had begun with a rather slack labour market and relatively under-utilized capacity. It was not only in the economic situation, however, but also in the philosophy of incomes policy that a change had occurred. At first regarded as an instrument for securing short-term stability, the policy gradually turned into an instrument for controlling business cycles and promoting growth, thereby supplementing fiscal and monetary controls.

At the beginning of the 60s there were several stabilization agreements and price and wage freezes, each followed by a new wave of price increases. This development was due to several factors which were present in various combinations. Some of the measures taken were badly timed with respect to the business cycle, so that a rapid wage drift developed during the wage freezes and led to high demands from the Trade Unions. In addition wage negotiations were often complicated by accompanying sudden increases in official prices, which were not synchronized with an upswing in the economy and/or with seasonal trends and so triggered off secondary price effects.

Developments were very different in the second half of the sixties. The Trade Unions then pursued a counter-cyclical wages policy and even conducted a round of negotiations in the slump. The timing and extent of wage movements were regulated by the so-called "Big Bargain" between both sides of industry, the Government and the National Bank, and under this (partly tacit) agreement employers and workers undertook to exercise restraint in wage and price demands, while in return the Government agreed to reduce taxation and the National Bank agreed to an easier credit policy. This agreement laid the foundation for the balanced and enduring upswing of recent years, which was for long accompanied by remarkable stability. In the last few years official price policy also has been essentially counter-cyclical and less spasmodic. Signs have appeared, however, that there are limits to the use of officially controlled prices as an instrument of counter-cyclical policy, since the unexpectedly prolonged upswing led to undue pressure on controlled prices, which eventually had to be raised before the boom had taken a definite downturn.

The technical efficiency of Austrian prices and incomes policy is far from perfect. The Joint Commission's price controls cover only certain commodities; the data on which decisions are made are insufficient; it is only possible to curb price increases, as also wage increases, to a small extent; and only few sanctions can be imposed. As has been explained, however, it is less important to perfect the controls than to use them properly and in particular to ensure correct timing (excluding, of course, emergency situations). The Joint Commission could in fact have staggered price and wage increases, while with the existing voluntary price controls it would have been possible for the Trade Unions to subordinate their wages policy to national economic considerations, although at the expense of maintaining the status quo in incomes distribution and of levelling up wage rates by increasingly paying above standard rates.

It is hard to establish whether Austrian prices and incomes policy was only able to prevent price explosions and postpone price increases in a few cases, or whether it succeeded in keeping down prices in general. A recent econometric study by the IMF found the irrelevance of inflationary expectations in Austria and concluded that this demonstrated the success of incomes policy. It is very likely that the counter-cyclical wages policy of recent years (by promoting consumption during slumps and investment during booms) has helped, not only to keep demand steady, but also to speed up economic growth. By ensuring monetary stability and continuous growth the prices and incomes policy has also strengthened the balance of payments and promoted full employment. Nor should its important contribution to the preservation of industrial peace be overlooked.

Table 1.　GROWTH

AVERAGE ANNUAL GROWTH RATE PER CENT

	REAL GNP			REAL GNP PER INHABITANT			REAL GNP PER EMPLOYED PERSON		
	60/65	65/70	60/70	60/65	65/70	60/70	60/65	65/70	60/70
Austria	4.4	5.1	4.7	3.5	4.7	4.1	4.4	5.7	5.0
Sweden	5.3	3.9	4.6	4.6	3.1	3.8	4.3	3.0	3.7
Switzerland	5.3	3.8	4.6	3.1	2.7	2.9	2.5	3.4	3.1
Great Britain	3.4	2.2	2.8	2.6	1.7	2.1	2.6	2.7	2.7
EFTA	4.1	3.2	3.6	3.2	2.6	2.9	3.3	3.2	3.2
Belgium	5.1	4.6	4.9	4.4	4.1	4.2	4.2	4.0	4.1
Netherlands	5.0	5.2	5.1	3.6	4.0	3.8	3.4	4.4	4.0
Italy	5.3	6.0	5.7	4.3	5.3	4.8	6.4	6.3	6.3
Germany	5.0	4.6	4.8	3.6	3.6	3.6	4.3	4.6	4.4
EEC	5.3	5.3	5.3	4.1	4.6	4.4	5.0	5.0	5.0
OECD in Europe	5.0	4.7	4.9	3.8	3.8	3.8	4.5	4.4	4.5
OECD	5.2	4.5	4.9	3.9	3.5	3.7	4.2	3.4	3.9

SOURCES: OECD and ILO.

34

Table 2. EMPLOYMENT AND LABOUR MARKET

| | EMPLOYED PERSONS | | | RATE OF UNEMPLOYMENT | | |
| | AVERAGE ANNUAL GROWTH RATE PER CENT | | | AVERAGE PER CENT | | |
	60/65	65/70	60/70	60/65	65/70	60/70
Austria	0.0	-0.6	-0.3	2.9	2.7	2.8
Sweden	1.0	0.9	0.9	1.3	1.6	1.5
Switzerland	2.7	0.4	1.5			
Great Britain	0.8	0.5	0.1	1.8	2.2	2.0
EFTA	0.8	0.0	0.4			
Belgium	0.9	0.6	0.8	3.4	3.3	3.4
Netherlands	1.5	0.8	1.1	0.6	1.4	1.0
Italy	-1.0	-0.3	-0.6	3.3	3.5	3.4
Germany	0.7	0.0	0.4	0.8	1.1	1.0
EEC	0.3	0.3	0.3			
OECD in Europe	0.5	0.3	0.4			
OECD	1.0	1.1	1.0			

SOURCE: ILO, OECD.

Table 3. PRICES AND COSTS

	GNP DEFLATOR			CONSUMER PRICES			LABOUR COSTS PER UNIT OF PRODUCTION (INDUSTRY)		
	60/65	65/70	60/70	60/65	65/70	60/70	60/65	65/70	60/70
			AVERAGE ANNUAL GROWTH RATE PER CENT						
Austria	4.1	3.3	3.7	3.9	3.3	3.6	3.6	2.0	2.8
Sweden	3.9	4.4	4.1	3.6	4.4	4.0	2.9	3.1	3.0
Switzerland	4.6	4.1	4.3	3.2	3.5	3.3	5.2	2.4	3.8
Great Britain	3.5	4.7	4.1	3.5	4.6	4.1	3.1	4.7	3.9
EFTA	3.9	4.7	4.3						
Belgium	3.0	3.7	3.3	2.5	3.5	3.0	2.6	2.6	2.6
Netherlands	4.8	5.4	5.1	3.6	4.9	4.3	6.0	3.3	4.6
Italy	5.3	3.6	4.4	4.9	2.9	3.9	6.2	3.7	4.9
Germany	3.6	3.5	3.5	2.8	2.7	2.7	4.2	3.3	3.7
EEC	4.2	3.9	4.1						
OECD in Europe	4.1	4.1	4.1	3.7	3.9	3.8			
OECD	2.7	4.2	3.4	2.4	4.2	3.3			

SOURCE: OECD and ECE.

Table 4. WAGES IN MANUFACTURING INDUSTRY

	HOURLY EARNINGS			WAGE RATES			WAGE DRIFT		
	60/65	65/70	60/70	60/65	65/70	60/70	60/65	65/70	60/70
	AVERAGE ANNUAL GROWTH RATE PER CENT						AVERAGE PER CENT		
Austria	9.2	8.0	8.6	6.5	7.2	6.9	2.7	0.8	1.7
Sweden	8.4	8.9	8.6	3.4	4.9	4.2	5.0	.0	4.4
Switzerland	7.5	6.5	7.0	5.5	5.2	5.3	2.0	1.3	1.7
Great Britain	5.9	7.6	6.8	4.5	6.7	5.6	1.4	0.9	1.2
EFTA									
Belgium	8.0	8.2	8.1	7.4	7.3	7.4	0.6	0.9	0.7
Netherlands	11.0	9.6	10.3	9.6	8.9	9.2	1.4	0.7	1.1
Italy	10.7	9.4	10.1	10.4	8.2	9.3	0.3	1.2	0.7
Germany	9.5	7.4	8.5	7.9	7.2	7.6	1.6	0.2	0.9
EEC									

SOURCE: OECD.

37

Table 5. BALANCE OF PAYMENTS

	FOREIGN BALANCE AS A PERCENTAGE OF GNP ANNUAL AVERAGES			PERCENTAGE OF IMPORTS COVERED BY CURRENCY RESERVES (PER CENT PER YEAR)			
	60/65	65/70	60/70	1960	1965	1970
Austria	0.0	-0.7	-0.4	49.5	58.3	49.5
Sweden	-0.2	-1.0	-0.5	16.7	19.2	10.9
Switzerland	-2.1	1.6[1]	-0.2[2]	105.0	89.2	72.7
Great Britain	-0.3	0.1	-0.1		18.3	13.0
Belgium	0.2	1.0	0.6	35.8	30.8	25.1
Netherlands	1.0	-0.1	0.4	38.3	27.5	24.2
Italy	0.8	2.1	1.2	65.0	57.5	35.5
Germany	1.1	2.4	1.7	66.7	36.7	45.6

1. 65/69.
2. 60/69

SOURCE: OECD, EEC.

Table 6. LABOUR DISPUTES

	NUMBER OF LABOUR DISPUTES			WORKERS INVOLVED (IN '000)			WORKING DAYS LOST (IN '000)		
	60/65	66/70	60/70	60/65	66/70	60/70	60/65	66/70	60/70
				ANNUAL AVERAGE					
Austria	.	.	.	80.0	31.3	57.8	175.2	27.9	108.2
Sweden	17	45	28	1.7	13.1	6.9	14.8	124.2	64.5
Switzerland	3	2	2	0.3	0.1	0.2	13.0	1.3	7.7
Great Britain	2,486	2,691	2,579	1,395.3	1,400.2	1,397.5	3,137.5	5,540.2	4,229.6
Belgium	45	88	65	21.8	48.2	33.8	243.1	534.9	375.8
Netherlands	68	33	52	24.0	16.4	20.6	106.2	63.4	86.8
Italy	3,467	3,274	3,379	2,865.8	4,044.7	3,401.6	11,644.9	17,667.6	14,886.6
Germany	.	.	.	74.1	110.9	90.9	410.1	156.9	295.0

SOURCE: ILO.

Table 7. GROWTH AND EMPLOYMENT
(Austria)

	REAL GNP	REAL GNP PER INHABITANT	REAL GNP PER PERSON EMPLOYED	OUTPUT PER PERSON EMPLOYED[1]	PERSONS EMPLOYED	UNEMPLOYMENT RATE PER CENT	UNEMPLOYED PER VACANCY
		ANNUAL RATE OF CHANGE PER CENT					
1960	5.6	5.0	5.0	1.4	0.5	3.5	2.8
1961	2.6	2.0	2.9	1.1	-0.2	2.7	1.7
1962	4.2	3.5	4.4	6.2	-0.2	2.7	1.7
1963	6.2	5.5	5.9	7.6	0.3	2.9	1.9
1964	3.4	2.9	3.8	4.1	-0.3	2.7	1.7
1965	5.0	4.5	5.5	5.0	-0.5	2.7	1.6
1966	2.4	1.9	3.6	4.1	-1.1	2.5	1.4
1967	4.4	3.9	5.7	8.9	-1.2	2.7	2.0
1968	6.1	5.6	6.4	8.8	-0.3	2.9	2.6
1969	7.8	7.4	7.6	4.8	0.2	2.8	2.0
1970	5.2	4.8	3.9	4.5	1.3	2.4	1.3
1971						2.1	1.0
60/65	4.4	3.5	4.1	4.0	0.0	2.9	1.9
65/70	5.1	4.7	5.7	6.3	-0.6	2.7	1.8
60/70	4.7	4.1	4.9	5.2	-0.3	2.8	1.9

1. In industry.

Table 8. PRICES, COSTS AND BALANCE OF PAYMENTS
(Austria)

	GNP DEFLATOR	INTERNAL DEMAND DEFLATOR	CONSUMER PRICE INDEX	LABOUR COSTS INDUSTRY	LABOUR COSTS OVERALL ECONOMY	FOREIGN BALANCE AS % OF GNP	CURRENT BALANCE (IN MILLIARDS SCHILLINGS)	IMPORT COVERAGE [1] (PER CENT)
	AVERAGE ANNUAL GROWTH RATE PER CENT							
1960	4.9	4.5	3.6	7.5	5.7	-0.5	-2.03	49.5
1961	3.8	3.6	4.4	5.4	6.6	0.7	1.54	55.0
1962	3.4	3.5	2.7	-0.2	3.7	0.9	4.39	67.5
1963	3.2	3.0	3.8	1.5	3.6	0.2	3.18	70.8
1964	5.3	5.1	5.0	4.6	6.0	-0.6	2.37	66.7
1965	3.0	2.9	2.2	6.6	4.9	-1.2	-1.20	58.3
1966	3.3	3.4	4.0	3.4	6.0	-2.4	-3.97	52.5
1967	2.4	2.2	2.8	-2.1	1.2	-1.4	4.00	59.2
1968	3.4	4.1	3.1	-2.3	2.2	-0.8	2.70	60.0
1969	4.4	5.1	4.4	4.3	1.2	0.8	1.93	54.2
1970	5.6	5.4	4.7	9.6	9.6	0.2	0.15	49.5
1971						-0.2	-2.72	50.0
60/65	4.1	4.0	3.9	3.7	5.1	0.0	1.38	61.3
65/70	3.3	3.6	3.3	1.9	3.1	-0.7	0.60	55.6
60/70	3.7	3.8	3.6	2.8	4.1	-0.4	1.18	58.5

1. Percentage of annual imports covered by currency reserves.

41

Table 9. WAGES AND DISTRIBUTION
(Austria)

| | INDUSTRIAL WORKERS | | HOURLY EARNINGS | AVERAGE EARNINGS PER EMPLOYED PERSON IN ALL SECTORS | | WAGES QUOTA [1] | WAGES QUOTA CORRECTED FOR STRUCTURAL CHANGE [2] |
	WAGE RATES	WAGE DRIFT		NOMINAL	REAL		
	AVERAGE ANNUAL GROWTH RATE PER CENT						
1960						59.0	59.0
1961	6.4	4.1	10.5	10.1	6.3	59.7	59.2
1962	5.0	3.8	8.8	8.7	4.1	61.3	60.3
1963	5.6	1.2	6.8	8.1	5.3	61.6	60.5
1964	5.1	3.8	8.9	9.1	5.1	62.1	60.6
1965	10.7	0.1	10.8	8.9	3.7	63.0	60.9
1966	6.5	1.6	8.1	9.7	7.3	64.6	61.9
1967	6.9	0.5	7.4	9.6	5.4	65.7	62.9
1968	6.9	-1.0	5.9	6.7	3.8	66.5	63.5
1969	5.7	0.7	6.4	7.8	4.6	65.6	62.0
1970	10.1	2.2	12.3	7.6	3.1	64.2	60.1
1971	11.1	2.0	13.1	12.2	7.2	66.1	60.9
60/65	6.5	2.7	9.2	9.0	4.8	61.1	60.1
65/70	7.2	0.8	8.0	8.3	4.9	64.9	61.9
60/70	6.9	1.7	8.6	8.6	4.8	63.0	61.0

1. Percentage share of wages and salaries in the national income.
2. Keeping the ratio constant between self-employed persons and persons in dependent employment, Base 1960.

Table 10. STRUCTURAL DATA
(Austria)

	1960	1965	1970
Percentage contribution to real GNP			
Agriculture	10.5	8.1	7.7
Industry[1]	47.2	49.2	50.8
Services	42.3	42.7	41.5
Percentage of gainfully employed in:			
Agriculture	24.2	20.7	17.3
Industry[1]	39.7	40.2	40.2
Services	36.1	39.1	42.5

1. Including the building and construction trades and electric power supply.

43

Table 11.   STRUCTURAL DATA
(Austria)

	1960	1970
	PER CENT	
Wages and salaries	59.0	63.6
Income from property and entrepreneurship	31.4	27.3
Agriculture	9.4	5.2
Other	22.0	22.1
Undistributed company profits	10.2	9.9
State income from property and entrepreneurship	0.8	0.7
Interest on national debt	-1.1	-1.5
National income	100.0	100.0

44

Part III

EVALUATION OF THE AUSTRIAN SYSTEM

by

Derek Robinson
Magdalen College, Oxford

INTRODUCTION

Dr. Suppanz has given a detailed description of the various administrative measures and parts of machinery that exist in order to exercise
some degree of influence or control over prices and wages. He has also
set out and commented on various analyses of the economic effects and
results of these measures. The intention of this paper therefore is not
to discuss the factual situation, machinery or the quantifiable economic
consequences or results. Rather it is to provide a personal view of how
the system appears to work to an outsider and to consider the implica-
tions and lessons that the Austrian experience might have for other
countries.

There is no widespread claim in Austria that a prices and incomes
policy, as that term is usually understood, exists. Some hold the view
that no policy can claim to be an incomes policy unless it seeks to influence all forms of income in approximately the same way and to the
same extent. Others believe that a prices and incomes policy implies
a degree of direct government intervention which would be either un-
desirable or harmful, or both, but which is in any event not apparent in
Austria. Nevertheless, it is clear that there are a variety of methods
and institutions whereby some degree of influence is brought to bear
on wage and, particularly, price determination over considerable areas
of the economy. Some of these are compulsory stemming from legislative
provisions, and others are the result of the voluntary agreement and co-
operation of the social partners and government, on the various committees and commissions that exist.

We will refer to the collection of methods and measures as a wage-price policy in order to recognize the distinction made by a number of people in Austria between this and an incomes policy in a more usual sense, and also to emphasize that there is nevertheless a policy for influencing the development of prices and to a lesser extent wages. The existence of the special, indeed unique, Chambers, creates conditions conducive to discussion and potential co-operation between powerful representative bodies well-financed and equipped with staff able to speak with authority and knowledge. While these institutions are unique and play an important part in the collection of policies and actions which together create an environment of influence and change on price and wage developments in Austria, it is nevertheless considered that they are neither sufficient nor necessary conditions for the creation and application in other countries of the sort of policy of co-operative approach to wage-price and economic policy generally that exists in Austria.

Austrian wage-price policy can be best understood if it is seen as part of a general broader approach to participation in economic and social policy-making rather than as a series of measures specifically designed to restrict the rate of increase in prices and money wages in accordance with some quantifiable criteria or guidelines. The general paraphernalia associated with quantifiable policies are absent in Austria. This means that it is not possible to apply the usual type of statistical tests to ascertain whether or not the policy has been successful. The policy is not seen as having a series of precisely-specified quantified objectives. Discussion of the size of the 'norm' or the exact wording of exception clauses or the amount by which certain wage or price changes can exceed the average is not only absent but generally regarded as alien to the basic underlying philosophy of the broad approach. Equally there is in general an absence of legalistically-based, or legalistically-biased, machinery to implement the policy although there are a number of direct controls on prices. However, as will be argued below it may be that there are pressures existing, or at least emerging in embryonic form, for change. This pressure is for greater government involvement which would possibly lead to greater specificity in the policy content and application.

THE MACHINERY AND CONTENT
OF THE WAGE-PRICE POLICY

The central influence on wage-price policy lies with the Joint Commission and its subordinate bodies, and indeed for wages this is effectively the only formal instrument of policy. However there are informal aspects. The trade union representatives on the Commission and the representatives from the Chamber of Labour, who are often trade unionists in another capacity, discuss the sort of general wage increases that are consistent with the prevailing and expected economic conditions and compatible with desirable social and economic policies. Prices are influenced by the Commission but also in some cases more directly by government intervention and legal price control.

In some cases the Minister can intervene to fix prices statutorily only if the four parties represented on the agency concerned unanimously agree that his intervention is desirable. In the past such unanimous agreement has not been forthcoming. Recently the Chamber of Trade and Industry has agreed that it will not exercise its veto right to prevent the Minister intervening and imposing statutory price controls in certain cases, particularly where the firm concerned has ignored the price rules adopted by the Commission. In general, however, the most marked feature of the Austrian institutions as seen by an observer influenced by British or American experience, has been the lack of formal machinery, the absence of detailed rules and provisions, and the great reliance on voluntariness and co-operation.

The Commission meets monthly, but the formal meetings are preceded by informal meetings of the chairmen of the four organisations – the three Chambers and the Trade Union Federation. It is at this preliminary meeting that the essential give-and-take of bargaining takes place. The staff of the organisations meet frequently both as officials of their respective organisations, meeting to prepare common ground and produce documents for their organisations' representatives on the Commission and various other bodies, and also as specialists in their own right, meeting to prepare background documents and analyses of the different economic and social problems. They therefore not only meet formally and informally but also relatively frequently. They meet on different committees in different guises performing different functions or as representatives of their parent organisation on various bodies. This is the case for both representative members or leaders and for officials and staff. There is a great interlocking and overlapping of representation on various bodies which means that the people concerned know each other well, meet frequently, recognize that they have to live together and are at the same time in a position to offset concessions or gains in one area with changes elsewhere.

The forms of organisations developed and the reappearance of a number of individuals on various different but inter-related committees and bodies means that it is possible for the people concerned to take a more comprehensive approach to their decision-taking than would be the case were each committee self-contained in the sense that members responsible for, say, discussing wage increases, were not also likely to meet elsewhere to discuss taxation policy, credit policy, the investment policy of the economy or some similar topic. The coverage of a committee or body influences but does not necessarily determine what that committee can effectively do. If the members of a committee know that they are also members of some other body dealing with a related or even different subject, they may well be influenced in their decisions in any one committee or organisation by their experience or expectations of results in another. This is why the interlocking and overlapping membership of the various parts of the machinery and institutions for discussing social and economic questions in Austria is so important. It permits a far broader view to be taken of any particular issue; each problem can be seen in its appropriate setting and solutions need be neither narrow nor short-term.

Wage bargaining is subject to very little direct intervention by Government. The two social partners carry out collective bargaining generally on an industry or sector basis within a framework of centralized influence. The Trade Union Federation exercises some influence on the timing of wage claims through discussions between trade union leaders, and also perhaps some lesser influence on the size of wage claims and settlements. It is not clear however whether, or to what extent, influence is exercised on the latter aspect. Understandably perhaps, neither individual trade unions nor the central organisation are particularly enthusiastic about discussing this sort of influence. This is a general problem with any form of wage or incomes policy which requires co-ordinated action by the trade union movement. Individual unions are not eager to express publicly that some claim which might have been put forward by their members has been modified because of pressure or consideration emanating from outside the union concerned, even though the source was the trade union movement as a whole.

Such influence as is exerted is on the whole confined to the industry-wide settlement. It appears to be commonly accepted that wage drift is the result of market forces rather than institutional behaviour and cannot therefore be subject to control by trade union actions or even by the concerted action of the social partners. As different industries pursue different policies regarding their industry-wide wage bargaining, so that some expect the larger part of all wage increases to come from the central settlement while others expect there to be a number of company bargains to supplement the central agreement, it is to be expected that the incidence of wage drift, insofar as this is measured on a British method, will vary from industry to industry.* Some of the apparent

* "British calculations would express drift as the difference in the percentage increase in wage rates and actual earnings thus implying the continuation of the proportionate status quo in terms of the relationship between rates and earnings at the base date. The Swedish method calculates each settlement afresh and so is not influenced by past drift, i.e. wage gap. The earnings figures would be adjusted for changes in overtime. For further discussion see Derek Robinson, "Wage drift, fringe benefits and manpower distribution", pp. 27-32, OECD, 1968.

increase over and above the industry-wide settlement will be the second-tier bargaining at company level. However, insofar as there is wage drift as normally understood, it provides a possible source of conflict or challenge to the underlying philosophy of the comprehensive system of tripartite discussion, consultation and decision-taking. If unions and employers are unable to control a significant area of wage movements they are perhaps unable to provide sufficient advantages to government in return for government concessions elsewhere. Alternatively if wage drift is seen as the result of market forces and if wage drift is seen as threatening relative price stability or the balance of payments, there is a danger that governments will have no acceptable alternative but to ease the pressures in the labour market in order to modify wage drift.

That this might become an issue stems from the fact that the total package of arrangements and institutions in Austria rests upon a tripartite approach to general social and economic policy-making, even though wage determination is essentially bipartite. This is perhaps both the overwhelming strength and the potential weakness of the Austrian system of wage influence. The social partners, being free in all formal senses to negotiate such wage increases as they decide, are not faced with a series of quantified restrictions against which they can quibble and direct their attack. They do not spend their time seeking to evade the rules and regulations in the pursuit of their own joint sectional interest. Neither can either side of the bargaining table use government-determined regulations as arguments in negotiation. Whatever decision the social partners take is theirs and they are responsible for it. To the extent that they wish to see the continuation of the total system of government consultation with industry they are under some obligation to ensure that they do not by their own actions threaten the basic economic stability and so reduce the area of common approach and acceptance of basic social and economic objectives that the whole system of consultation is jeopardized. Thus they are under some obligation to accept some modification to their actions to the extent that the whole system might be threatened. This means that the basic attitude is not one of restraint and objection to irksome restrictions but rather one of voluntarily-imposed and accepted broad limitations on one's own freedom of action in order to preserve a general system which is considered worthwhile.

An important point to emphasize therefore is that while it is possible to point to specific institutions and administrative organisations and committees which might be aggregated to provide the machinery of wage-price policy these various institutions in themselves do not satisfactorily explain the total apparatus and environment. The whole is greater than the sum of the parts. Each piece of the framework or totality of institutional framework and environment remains operative and supported because it is in part at least regarded as a piece of supporting infrastructure for the whole system.

Trade unions have not only traditionally relied on bargaining as the way of achieving their objectives; it is also the preferred way. As a general universal principle free trade unions prefer bargaining as the means of determining terms and conditions of employment and of exercising their influence. In usual wage negotiations bargaining takes place between the two social partners or representatives of workers and employers. They take such decisions as they can mutually agree upon influenced by considerations of their own interests. The resulting decision is intended to satisfy the interests and objectives of those who are party to it, and while any particular decision may influence other decisions, either, for example, through the processes of coercive comparisons on other wage settlements or through unit costs on product prices, these are not regarded by the two parties as of much immediate concern to them unless and to the extent that their own interests, individually or jointly, are affected. They accept responsibility for their own decisions but feel little obligation to take account of other people's interests.

At the same time if trade unions wish to exert influence on government policy they may have to choose between different approaches. In some countries they attach themselves to a political party, or may even have taken the original initiative in establishing a party. Elsewhere they may have but loose attachments to any single party but prefer to support specific measures no matter which party introduces them and to advocate support for different parties at different times.

Trade unions also wish to exercise influence over a wider area than the terms and conditions of employment which are the subject of their bipartite collective bargaining. They recognize that the real benefits and value of their negotiated conditions can be considerably influenced by government action in, say, the field of fiscal policy. In some cases they choose, or circumstances compel them, to recognise that certain objectives can only, or can best, be obtained through the state rather than by bipartite collective bargaining, as, for example, health services, high and stable employment, opportunities for training and retraining. There are other areas which can only be effectively covered by government action or for which it is now accepted that government should shoulder prime responsibility such as general growth trend, distribution or redistribution of income and relatively stable prices. In short it can be asserted that trade unions are now aware that certain of their objectives - and these may be in effect the relatively narrow ones usually covered by collective bargaining but translated into real as opposed to nominal or money terms, or they may be the broader aspects of social economic policy - can essentially be provided only by government. The possible objectives that can be attained by bi-partite collective bargaining between the two social partners are limited to those areas which are within the area of effective control by the social partners In modern societies this area is diminishing. It diminishes as a result

50

of increased government intervention in, and responsibility for, more and more issues. In part this increase in the area of concern and responsibility of government may be due to demands emanating from the trade unions themselves. The pressure for high and sustained levels of employment comes not least from trade unions and it follows that if governments are expected to provide or create certain conditions they must be enabled to exercise the degree of influence or control necessary for the attainment of those conditions.

In some ways therefore trade unions are increasingly seeking to obtain from governments changes or policies which are desirable in themselves or which create environmental conditions in which the unions can more easily or more actively pursue their objectives. Governments in turn require certain pre-conditions and behavioural patterns from various groups in society if they in turn are to be able to satisfy the various and competing demands made on government. For example in order to provide conditions conducive to high and stable growth with full employment, the government may require relative price stability which may imply certain modifications in the behaviour of workers, trade unions and employers. The social partners and government may see the process of discussion and consultation necessary for the exposition of the objectives and priorities of various groups, the changes necessary in order to remove incompatibilities in the demands of different groups, and the co-ordination of the various threads of economic activity as a continuous process of bargaining. Trade unions are certainly more likely to see it in this way. Trade unions are above all else bargainers. It is their preferred way of conducting their affairs, defended not only because it has often appeared to serve well the interests of trade unions in the results that have been obtained, but also because it is desired as a method of conducting affairs which is considered superior to alternatives such as the imposition of decisions by outside bodies or agencies.

There is nothing new or unusually novel therefore in the notion that unions and employers might indulge in a form of bargaining with government in order to determine priorities, discover the extent of mutual objectives and common ground, and to consider what changes in behaviour might be necessary in order to satisfy the objectives of some other group or as a 'reasonable' price to be paid for the achievement of some desired objective. Indeed it is suggested that in most, if not all free countries, there is some extent to which unions, employers and government indulge in some form of bargaining over national policies and priorities. This 'bargaining' may be only slightly developed and consist of little more than periodic consultation and discussion, or an established informal system may have grown up which, despite its lack of formal agreement and its apparently haphazard or casual nature, may nevertheless be the crucial area of discussion and agreement and provide the essentially formal part of the institutional machinery.

One of the important features of the recognition of the existence of such a tripartite bargaining arrangement or of the need to develop clearer lines of communication, is the acceptance of areas of mutual interest and concern and the realization that restraint on one's own actions in some areas may be a necessary condition for success in other areas. As with orthodox collective bargaining on a bipartite basis, complete victory is rare; most decisions are compromises. The development of a system of tripartite consultation, discussion and in a way ultimate decision-taking has gone a long way in Austria.

Thus the existence of the various bodies such as the Advisory Council on Social and Economic Problems allows the social partners to participate in discussions on the broader social and economic questions, but the current existence of these institutions does not in itself explain their creation and survival. In part this is the result of the recent history of Austria which itself partly accounts for, as well as includes, the existence of the coalition government for so long a period. The position of Austria politically has also contributed to a somewhat special attitude towards co-operation and government by general consensus. While these features may be especially marked in their incidence in Austria they are not uniquely Austrian. Other countries too have had periods of considerable co-operation between the social partners and tripartite discussions or 'bargaining' leading to the establishment of fairly wide areas of common ground between them. But this has apparently lasted longer and thrives more strongly in Austria than elsewhere. It is this underlying belief in and acceptance of the broad areas of common ground and the general support of what we will describe as government by general consensus that explains why the Austrians have been able to continue to exercise their wage-price policy for as long as they have.

The policy has been possible because of the existence of other conditions. It did not itself create the conditions of co-operation, nor did the extension of discussion and bargaining to wider areas of social and economic policy develop in response to trade unions demanding a quid pro quo for their reduced autonomy in bargaining over money wage increases with the perceived consequential loss of independence and power. This is perhaps what is specially important about Austria; that the development of a wage-prices policy was possible because of the existence of other practices and habits connected with economic policy decision-taking. The creation of machinery to deal specifically with wages and prices could therefore be seen as an extension and continuation of attitudes and practices already established, rather than as the injection of a sharp shock which challenged the autonomy of the social partners and raised fears of excessive governmental intervention in what were regarded as areas of decision-taking traditionally the preserve of the two social partners alone acting in concert through orthodox collective bargaining.

This then is what is seen as the content and machinery of wage-price policy: self-restraint exercised within a broad framework of tripartite discussion and 'government by consensus'. The informal machinery and attitudes developed therefrom are far more important than the formal apparatus, although the existence of the legal provisions for certain forms of price control is important as an indicator of government's intentions.

The purpose or objective of the policy is much more concerned with general economic conditions than with prices and wages alone. Thus the emphasis on the wage front is given to anti-cyclical wage settlements rather than to purely anti-inflationary settlements. Indeed it is considered that some degree of inflation is inevitable in a fully-employed economy. The important question is the rate of inflation, and this is decided more by general discussion and agreement informally than by a formal declaration that inflation of a given amount has been accepted for the coming period and built in to the economic policies. Such an approach would lead inevitably into the quantifiable norms or guideposts approach to which Austrian opinion appears to be so strongly opposed. Whether or not the policy is in fact anti-cyclical will be considered below.

HAS THE POLICY WORKED?

To determine whether a wage-price policy has been successful it is necessary to specify the objectives and decide on acceptable criteria by which their attainment, or failure to attain them, can be measured. In so far as the question of reducing wage and price inflation is concerned, there are basically two kinds of tests. We can select internal or external criteria.

Internal criteria require that there be some view as to what would have happened to prices in the absence of the wage-price policies but in otherwise similar economic circumstances. This pre-supposes the existence of some relatively fixed relationships between quantifiable variables of the general form of what has become known as the Phillips curve. It may be that there is such a relationship for Austria which holds with sufficient constancy and consistency to permit decisions to be reasonably and reliably taken on the 'performance' of the economy in any one year. But if there is, it must be derived from the past when similar sorts of wage-price policies operated and so it cannot tell us whether the present policy is working. It could only indicate whether it was working better or less effectively than it did in the past. This is not the same as the question of whether it ever worked. Also, of course, in practice, any general relationship of the Phillips curve type tends to have variation about the average relationships such that it is not really possible to assert with great confidence that in a particular year the packet of policies did or did not have a precise quantifiable effect.

External criteria require that we test the results of a collection of policies in one country against the results of a collection of policies - similar or different - in other countries. Thus, some people have argued that a prices and incomes policy in a specific country has not worked because that country has not had lower inflation than some other country which did not have a prices and incomes policy. In some ways this rests on the view that the underlying relationships between the economic variables included in the comparisons are similar, i.e. that there is a "natural" Phillips curve which shows the relationship that could be expected to hold in a number of countries at the same time. There appears to be no evidence for this view, but that does not, of course, necessarily prevent people from holding it. Rather, it would appear that the relationships, such as they are, vary from country to country.

Whether one adopts internal or external criteria it is necessary to make some assumptions about what would have happened had conditions been different from what they actually were, i.e. if there had been no wage-price policy. While this is to some extent a question of judgment and interpretation of data, the author's view is that there is no really satisfactory way of discovering what would have happened in an economy if some important variable had been different. It is suggested that to some extent the assessment of whether or not a prices and incomes policy is working depends on whether people believe that it is. It also, of course, depends on the objectives that are sought from the policy. Dr. Suppanz has produced a variety of evidence about internal and external facts that might be thought relevant if quantifiable criteria are sought. It is a matter of personal judgement how these are used and wha conclusions are drawn.

My overwhelming impression is that the Austrians themselves do not place much importance on quantifiable justification for prices-wages polic and would not seek to defend their collection of policy measures by reference to a statistical series. Rather they would emphasize the general climate. Thus not only is it difficult, if not impossible, to try and conclude whether the policy does or does not work, it is also difficult or impossible to say whether the trade unions or the employers should, from the viewpoint of their own sectional interests, continue to participate in the policy measures. All one can do is report that the social partners themselves appear convinced that the balance of advantage clearly lies in the continuation of the system.

Moreover they produced two strong arguments over and above the "reduction of inflation" points of view. They emphasized that they had a remarkable record of industrial peace and that their economic growth and employment level had been very stable on a comparative basis. On both counts the evidence is impressive.

Strikes seldom take place. There is a marked propensity to settle industrial disputes in a peaceful way. To some extent this may be because employers are reluctant to take a strong attitude of resistance to trade union claims and grant relatively high wage increases. The evidence as considered above would not appear to provide particularly strong support for this view, although, of course, there has been inflation and it is expected to continue. An alternative explanation could be that trade unions are weak and not able to exercise much industrial pressure in support of their claims and do not strike because they are not strong enough to do so. This would also appear to be contrary to the evidence. The impression obtained from discussion with the social partners is that there are few strikes because both parties prefer to use other methods of solving their differences of opinion, for even with government by consensus differences of opinion exist. The record of industrial peace is significant and valued. It is both evidence that the total system is working reasonably well and justification for the continuation of the system. For an important conclusion is that neither of the social partners really believes that its own interest, or the general interest would be better served by greater industrial unrest. Strikes seldom take place therefore because they are perceived as less desirable ways of determining wage increases than is the present system.

In relation to the second point, the relative stability of employment and economic growth, which seems to have been becoming more marked, can be taken to demonstrate that the collection of policies does have an effect, not necessarily on the inflation rate, but on the whole collection of economic conditions which together make up the real standard of living and economic environment of the community. In this case the contra-cyclical or stabilizing policies adopted by the unions might be seen as having an important reward in the protection of the employment conditions of their members. In any particular year wages might not have risen by as much as could have been obtained, but this is regarded as having been offset by the relatively higher increases obtained in other years when the economy would have gone into relative decline - e.g. the rate of growth would have been reduced, and possibly below that of the rate of increase in productivity, so leading to unemployment. For example the development of incomes since 1967, as set out by Dr. Suppanz, has been markedly contra-cyclical. Indeed the growth of wage drift during the expansionary years can be interpreted as market forces creating wage increases which had been denied by the institutional actions of the social partners. It was because the partners deliberately sought to restrict the rate of increase in wages that the relatively strong wage drift developed. Similarly this was offset by, or the counterpart to, an agreement that wages would continue to rise, albeit at a somewhat slower overall rate, during the less expansionary years.

One of the factors taken into account by unions in their contra-cyclical policy is that Government is willing to implement an active manpower policy which aims at employment creation and maintenance during the downswings of the cycle. This is something that the two social partners cannot themselves ensure and implement. Government co-operation is necessary and again illustrates the basically tri-partite nature of the totality of the whole system of government by consensus and agreement.

Equally there is evidence that the present Government is willing to produce a tax policy more favourable to wage and salary earners as part of the overall package of policy measures. Union wage claims both respond to this and exert some pressure on Government to introduce the appropriate sort of tax policies.

It is because they take a relatively comprehensive view about the scope of their bargaining and responsibilities that trade unions believe that such an approach is in their members' interests and the best way of improving the real standard of living. They place considerable emphasis on the fact that employment levels are maintained during the relatively bad years of the economic cycle, and believe that government intervenes in this respect, at least in part, because of the moral obligations imposed on any government involved in tripartite bargaining on a broad basis to provide satisfactory general economic and social conditions in return for which the social partners voluntarily surrender some of their autonomy in wage and price determination. The inter-connections of the adaptations in attitudes and behaviour are perhaps best seen in the wage-employment relationships and effects over the cycle and the development and greater emphasis of the stabilizing approach of trade unions which has gradually emerged as their confidence in government has increased. This may be the result of changes in the political character of the government. It may also be due to the changes in attitudes and expectations that naturally occur through time, or, perhaps, because of the recognition that even more voluntary co-operation was necessary. Whatever the cause, or causes, it would appear that over the past few years there has been a willingness to accept on a voluntary basis more restraints on wage and price increases at particular times, even though these are perhaps moderate and uncertain in origin or implementation.

That additional co-operation or further willingness to participate in tripartite-agreed but bipartite-applied actions on the wage front exists, might be taken as grounds for believing that previous policies

have not worked as they were too weak and ineffective. However, this
would be to understate the ways in which the policy is applied and to fail
to recognize the crucial role occupied by the informal approaches. The
need to strengthen the voluntary co-operation resulted in part from the
increasing pressures exerted on the Austrian economy from internal
expansion and external developments and from the changing demands on
the economy made by the social partners and their representatives.

In the last resort the question of whether the wage-price policy, or
indeed any form of incomes policy, has worked is a matter of judgement
and not something that can be discovered by the automatic processing
of particular series of statistics. In the Austrian case it is suggested
that the policy has worked; worked in the sense that parties to collective bargaining believe that their actions are influenced by developments
in policy elsewhere and that their own actions will influence the development of policies elsewhere. There is, in my opinion, an effect on the
central wage negotiations in that the decisions taken there are different
from those that would have been taken in the absence of the general
framework of policy-making. The clearest evidence of this is the contra-
cyclical wage policies recently developed. However there is less evidence that the social partners seek to contain wage drift as part of their
antagonistic co-operative approach.

RELATIONSHIPS WITH GOVERNMENT

The unusual features about the Austrian development when compared
with similar developments elsewhere is that this form of co-operative
tripartite bargaining has survived the demise of the political coalition.
In some other countries there may be less willingness by the trade
unions to continue their co-operative relationship with government once
'their' political party is no longer part of the government. This may be
because the unions believe that the government is no longer pursuing
policies designed to improve the position of trade union members either
as fast, or as much, as should be done, or that the government is giving
preferential treatment to other groups in society who in the view of trade
unions have far less social justice and equity to support their claims.
But Austrian experience has allowed the unions to continue their co-
operative approach even when the coalition ended because it was accepted
that there would still continue to be a minimum amount of common ground
between the government and the social partners, so as to ensure that
the benefits of co-operation outweighed the disadvantages that might result from embarking on a period of more antagonistic attitudes and approaches. Similarly the employers believe that it is possible to maintain the general relationships even though there is now a socialist

government in office. Thus there is a general acceptance of the view that even though the two social partners might each be linked to a particular political party, the co-operation originating with the Grand Coalition had some benefits which should be carried over to the party Government formation. It does not appear either inconsistent or unusual for each social partner to be associated with a different political party which opposes the other electorally, and yet for each of them to be committed to the general principle of government by consensus and co-operation, so that whatever the political government of the day the 'other' social partner is able to continue in broad co-operation and participation in the various institutions and bodies even though politically it might be actively supporting the current opposition party.

At first sight this may appear to an outsider to suggest that either trade unions or employers' associations, or both, have forfeited their traditional roles, to form a kind of corporate state. This would be wrong. Rather they have seen and encouraged a transformation of their roles, in the sense that they have altered not their functions, which are to defend and protect the interests of their members, but the way in which those functions are exercised. It could be interpreted as a recognition that in a modern industrial society all interests are inter-related and bound up with each other, and that class war on the old lines fighting the traditional battles is increasingly irrelevant and indeed probably harmful to the interests of one's own members. The particular view taken on this issue will depend on one's own value judgments and it is not the purpose of this paper to pass comment on the value judgments of others or to advocate any particular set of political or moral values. It is possible to say, however, that Austrian trade unionists who regarded themselves as socialists are convinced that this form of co-operative participation in what we have called government by general consensus is not only conducive to the achievement of their interests and to their members' advantage but also much to be preferred to alternative methods of operation. Thus, rather than emphasizing the restrictive nature of any constraints implied in the wage-price policy, the social partners tend more to emphasize the advantages to be received from the participation. This may be due to the fact that in the past the constraints have been relatively minor and innocuous and, on the whole, both voluntarily determined and applied, particularly on the wage side. Thus the trade-off between the autonomy of the two social partners on the one hand and the gains to be had by influencing government policies on the other was seen as being on rather favourable terms.

This could be subject to pressure. It is suggested that the Government will need to pay increasing attention to price inflation. There is a growing public concern against inflation. This appears to be a widespread phenomenon observable in a number of countries. The public not only now want to see a reduction in the rate of inflation but they place the prime responsibility for initiating action to obtain this result firmly on government. In turn, governments, reactive to public views, are devoting greater attention to ways of reducing the inflationary pressures while maintaining high levels of employment and economic growth. They are in many cases paying more attention to prices and incomes policies than they may have done in the more recent past. There is a wide search for ways of reconciling the various aims of government in the social and economic field and incomes policies is one of the possibilities being considered or reconsidered.

This is one reason why the present government in Austria has increased its participation in the activities of the Joint Commission, particularly on the price front. It is playing a more directly positive role than it has at certain periods in the past and will probably continue to do so. In addition the political nature of the government no doubt encourages it to increase its direct concern. Socialist governments might well be expected to be more willing as well as more disposed to direct intervention on prices and when this is taken alongside the perceived increasing attention and concern about price increases on the part of the public generally it might not be unreasonable to suppose that even further direct intervention by government might be expected or forthcoming.*

If government does seek to exert more direct pressure on the social partners in order to reduce price inflation it is likely that the foundations of the basic voluntaryism of the policy and the associated broader-based co-operation will come under increased pressures and strains. It is not clear whether the system will be able to withstand additional pressure and still maintain its framework of government by general consensus, as part of that general consensus is the acceptance of the voluntary nature of the series of arrangements. It is possible that if additional pressure is exerted on one part of the total arrangements for general tripartite discussion and decision-taking the whole edifice will be threatened. This would be so if it were the case that the existing arrangements work because they recognize that there are limitations that can be imposed on the social partners in the pursuance of their basic functions of price and wage determination, and that if attempts are made to push them beyond the limits of what is to them politically and effectively possible and practical, the end result will be that they will withdraw from participation rather than risk jeopardizing their fundamental relationships with their constituent members or take the chance of overstraining the voluntary co-operation. If it is thought that there is a margin within which willing and co-operative social partners can influence wage and price decisions by their voluntary actions and co-operation, but that there are also real limitations to that margin beyond which attempts to constrain the responses of the partners to either economic forces or the

* It is emphasized that this is entirely my personal opinion.

59

pressures emanating from within their own organisations are bound to fail, and in failing to lead to a situation even worse than would exist without the attempts at wage-price policy at all, then there is a real danger in trying to obtain more restraint than the situation can be expected to yield. This is a danger faced by all governments which seek to implement a policy based upon, or which incorporates, an element of voluntaryism.

It is not suggested that the Austrian government has sought to exceed the possible limits of voluntaryism nor that it seeks to do so. But the possibility of this occurring is a real one particularly in the light of the growing public concern that the rate of increase in prices should be brought under control. If the government is to be loaded with the responsibility for certain economic situations, it is reasonable to suppose that it will seek to obtain powers effectively to deal with that situation. In this way governments can be 'compelled' to embark on aspects of policy which might not in abstract or in principle be attractive to them.

To some extent it is possible that additional powers might be taken against foreign-owned companies. This would fill in one of the more obvious weaknesses of the present system and avoid some of the more troublesome aspects of increasing the area of government intervention against domestic companies. If prognostications are permitted then it is probable that government will intervene here and so far as the domestic situation is concerned be more concerned to deepen rather than widen existing powers. But this too, as has been suggested, could raise problems of participation for the social partners. Institutions and attitudes and behaviour in Austria seem to reflect general public views and concern to a considerable extent and if it is correct to assume, as has been asserted above, that there has been a change in public attitude in that there is now greater concern over inflation than hitherto, then it is reasonable to expect that the existing institutions themselves will have to react to the changed conditions. It is less clear whether they will react in such a way as to accommodate the changed views within the existing broad framework of voluntaryism, or whether the increased direct intervention will so disturb the balance of power and the delicate mechanisms of interchange of view, and the processes by which decisions ultimately emerge, that the mechanisms cease to function. If the latter possibility is the more likely then it may be that the social partners will prefer to stand by the sectional interests of their constituents rather than modify their behaviour to adjust to the requirements of the new expression of the public interest. For while it is recognized that both trade unions and companies are part of the public interest it is also the case that these organisations need not necessarily, in the pursuit of their sectional interests, behave in ways which are consistent with the pursuit of the public good.

Impressions are that this danger is less in Austria than in most other countries, but as a possible danger it needs to be mentioned. What might perhaps happen is that the processes of decision-taking and consultation will be presented publicly with more extremism and contrast of view. Some of the disagreements which have taken place at the informal meetings might be brought into the open as disagreements rather more than in the past when they could well have been settled by compromise or in response to countervailing settlements offering offsetting advantages elsewhere. The emergence of party governments rather than coalition might encourage this. Ultimately the crucial question is whether the perceived benefits and disadvantages of the system outweigh the advantages and disadvantages of the next most-likely alternative. This is the justification for establishing the system in the first place and for its continuation.

If the government should seek to play a more positive or active part in the application of the policy this ought not to be regarded as being a major change of principle. The government is already heavily involved and the existing system is a tri-partite not a bi-partite system. The nature of the current tendencies, if they have been read and understood aright, is that the government might feel compelled to shift the emphasis somewhat between private and public involvement and also to obtain some realignment in the relative distribution of power. Whether the latter would be relatively slight and unimportant or whether it would be such as to challenge the basis of the tri-partite system, i.e. the agreed and accepted allocation and inter-dependence of decision-taking and consultation, remains to be seen.

If there is a change of emphasis it may more likely take the form of more overt direct intervention by government. Government has always been involved in the decision-taking processes in Austria, but has tended to hold itself in the background rather than present itself in the forefront of activity. This could give the impression that the government plays a passive role. However it might well be that the background intervention and the type of activities necessary to ensure that the discussions of the social partners in the various bodies and agencies are somehow or other capable of being combined into a comprehensive package of policies which are not inconsistent or contradictory, requires in fact a considerably more active government than is often supposed. The involvement of government is not necessarily indicated by the degree of publicity which attends government action nor by the apparent workings of a social and economic system. What Austrian governments will probably need in the future - and this is irrespective of their political complexion - is more depth to their existing powers both in order that they can the more effectively intervene in price and wage decisions when necessary, and, and this is at least as important, in order that they can be seen, openly and publicly, to be trying to react to the growing public concern over price inflation. Whether changes take place or not it should nevertheless be recognized that the role of government in a tri-partite bargaining situation, where the whole area of economic and social policy is within the scope of discussion and consultation, does require a positive attitude and involves the government in at least as much intervention as would occur in an orthodox relationship with the social partners. For just as the social partners are influenced to some extent by government decisions so is the government influenced by decisions of the social partners, and influenced in a positive way. It cannot merely seek to negate developments resulting from the decisions of the social partners on the grounds that these are contrary to the public interest as perceived by government for it becomes recognized as part of the system that the two social partners have a role to play in interpreting as well as transmitting views as to what the public interest is. Thus the decisions of the social partners have to be accommodated within the broad framework of government policy to a more marked degree. Yet government cannot merely blindly or automatically incorporate such decisions into its total policy measures. Inconsistencies and contradictions could well arise. It is necessary to ensure that a harmonious balance is maintained while also pursuing the specific objectives of government policy. This is what requires a positive role from government and why it is considered that the role of the Austrian government is in fact more active and interventionist than is often thought and than is often found in other countries.

LESSONS FOR OTHER COUNTRIES

It should not be expected that practices, institutions or attitudes from one country can be easily or painlessly transferred elsewhere even if it is decided that it would be desirable for them to be so transferred. At the same time the view that no experiences or lessons can be learned from other countries is equally extreme and misleading. The really difficult task is to decide which particular aspects are the important and desirable ones and how the beneficial results rather than the processes can be adopted.

The first choice to be made by a country that seeks to implement a prices and incomes policy is whether it should consist of quantifiable criteria, yardsticks, norms and guideposts which set out with some considerable degree of clarity, precision and rigour the limits within which prices and incomes should change, or whether the policy is instead to seek to exert a more indirect less quantifiable but nevertheless valuable influence on wage and price development. Austria has chosen the latter type and therefore countries seeking to introduce a detailed quantifiable policy might expect to find little of value in Austrian experience. This, however, would not be the case. While there might be little in the area of detailed application of a policy which would be of direct benefit, the lessons which can be derived from the general environmental situation are no less appropriate for countries wishing to pursue the one kind of incomes policy as for those seeking to introduce the other.

The major contribution made by Austrian experience is that it is possible for the social partners to agree on a broad framework of socio-economic policies which can in turn be the subject of discussion and consultation with government so that there emerges a broad consensus which receives wide support at least for its main outlines. The social partners themselves modify to some extent their own behaviour in the light of the requirements of government. The provision of numerous opportunities for representatives and staff officials of the social partners and various agencies of government to meet to discuss both major policy issues and the more technical aspects of the implementation of policy, cements the various pieces of machinery into a totality of institutions, arrangements and understandings which permit the creation of a coherent and comprehensive approach to a wide range of issues. This is crucial. The system rests on its inter-relationships and inter-dependencies.

Thus wage-price policy is not seen as a restrictive device intended to reduce the money (and by implication) the real incomes of employed persons. Rather it is seen as one, but only one, aspect of the wide range of methods available for influencing the development of the economy. This in part results from, and at the same time in part determines, the approaches to wage-price policy as a less important part of total policy. No great claims are made about the possible efficacy of wage policy. Indeed there is some reluctance to a claim that one exists. Consequently parts of the price policy have to be muted. Instead of a quantifiable policy there is the intention to exert some influence, as and when considered appropriate and possible, on the development of wages in a contra-cyclical manner. For some countries this might be considered insufficient, as indeed it has been suggested might prove to be the case in Austria. An attempt to take part of the Austrian system, that of tri-partite bargaining, for in essence the series of consultations and discussions between the social partners and government is a form of bargaining, and superimpose upon it a more rigorous form of wage policy with guidelines, norms and exception clauses, can hope to succeed only to the extent that it is possible to secure the agreement of the social partners to the stronger form of incomes policy.

A most important lesson therefore is that if a tripartite approach to deal with long-term problems is sought, it might be necessary to forgo the opportunity to obtain dramatic short-term gains which by the very act of their securance destroy the underlying goodwill and co-operation necessary for the establishment of tri-partite bargaining. The stresses and strains that can be placed on the system and the amount of direct contribution to an anti-inflationary policy that can be secured from a wage-price policy are therefore seen in pragmatic terms. A realistic view is taken of what is considered possible. This might be less than some policy-makers would require but in this sensitive area in which a choice must always be taken, it would seem that the Austrians have placed greater weight on realistic assessments of what is practical and possible than on what is considered ultimately desirable in terms of short-run direct contribution to policy.

Governments seeking to obtain this degree of participation by the social partners must be willing to amend and adjust their own policies in the light of representations and arguments from the partners. Essentially the process should be regarded as one of tri-partite bargaining on a higher level covering broader ground in somewhat less precise detail than traditional bi-partite collective bargaining and the associated system of pressuring government. An important part of the system is the involvement of individuals in a whole series of different but related activities. The overlapping membership of the various bodies is more than just accidental and more vital than might at first sight appear. It is one of the most important ways in which government by consensus operates. Common views and compromises emerge as part of the constant process of discussion.

The anticipated outside criticism would be that the price that each of the social partners pays for its participatory role in government by consensus is the abandonment, or at least serious weakening, of its individual position on issues of importance. Thus it might be argued that the trade unions have been induced to abandon their basic role of opposition in pursuit of an ephemeral participation in real decision-taking. Alternatively it might be said that employers have given up their right to follow pricing and investment policies best suited to their interests and the interests of their shareholders. In part the response to this sort of question, and even the raising of the questions themselves, is a matter of political views and judgments. What can be claimed however is that the social partners do not believe that they have abandoned any basic position affecting their principles or interests. Rather they take the view that they are modifying their traditional behavioural patterns in the light of a realistic reassessment and reinterpretation of the functions of employers and trade unions in a modern integrated industrial democratic society. Of course, they would recognize that they each accept certain basic philosophical positions such as a belief in Western democracy, the preservation of free trade unions and employers' associations, and the continuation of a mixed economy, even though different groups within the main divisions of the social partners may seek to change the relative mix of various components in the mixed economy. They would, however, reject the view that they had sacrificed their basic position as defenders of the particular interests of their members.

While it is a question of interpretation and personal judgement, my opinion is that the system practised in Austria has been the result of a realistic reappraisal of the practicalities of dealing with real hard problems in the conditions of a modern mixed economy in which the population seek full employment, fast and stable growth, social peace and, increasingly, more stable prices. The extent of public ownership may make Austria a somewhat peculiar example of a mixed economy, but it is thought that the essential understanding of the necessities of political action required for the successful application of a policy of government by consensus is more important. While there are differences of opinion about the distribution of the national product, not least between employment income and profits, the differences are resolved within a framework which each of the social partners recognizes as being essentially fair.

The basic attitudes are the crucial feature, but there are also institutions and administrative arrangements which are conducive to such success as Austria has enjoyed. The Chambers make a significant contribution, as does the existence of a structure of industrial trade union organisation. It has been suggested that the fact that Austria is a small country is also relevant. There is some weight to this point in that the administrative problems in a small country, any small country, are more likely to be more manageable than the administrative problems in larger countries. Moreover, the relative smallness of Austria enables the overlapping of membership of various committees to take place without the relatively few representatives becoming unrepresentative or isolated from their constituents. However smallness cannot be considered either a necessary or a sufficient condition. While all these factors make some contribution the overriding factor is that the partners and government recognize the value of offsetting concessionary bargaining over a wide area of social and economic policy. This is the feature that can most profitably be imported from Austria. The particular institutions may wither in foreign climates but this underlying basic philosophy must provide the root of any attempt to emulate Austrian experience and advantages by grafting on to existing national institutions a new set of attitudes.

The importance of the attitudinal actions and values is also the potential weakness of the Austrian system. Unlike institutions, attitudes exist only when people choose to maintain them. The emergence of party government may provide a challenge to the philosophy of government by consensus. In many other countries there is no experience of coalitions and little experience of genuine fundamental co-operation with political parties associated with the 'other' social partner. In these cases the basic attitudes may be more difficult to create. In the same way they may be challenged in Austria. This will be the hard test of the wage-price policy. It is probable that for the time being the social partners will decide that the total package of measures is a desirable one. Public opinion will no doubt react harshly to proposals that might appear to be increasing the risk of additional inflation. In the same way other countries might be encouraged to try and develop institutions and attitudes similar to those in Austria in the hope of reducing the inflationary problems facing them. They will be even more encouraged if their objectives give greater weight to the development of mutually-agreed tripartite social and economic policies.

In essence the lesson of Austria is that tripartite bargaining offers some prospects for the attainment of some of the objectives of the social partners and governments. The particular forms, machinery and administrative arrangements, are of less importance than the desire to achieve certain broad policy goals. That this is possible by the creation of a system of offsetting concessionary bargaining is apparent. Whether the quantifiable results in terms of price changes and moderation in inflationary pressure are considered sufficiently attractive to induce the social partners to modify their traditional behaviour and voluntarily surrender what they regard as essential freedoms in the pursuit of jointly-agreed goals is debatable. That there will be a continuation of the inflationary process, and/or a serious threat to employment levels, leading to general dissatisfaction with both the results and the continuation of the existing system itself if nothing is done, appears both obvious and a matter for urgent consideration. It is in this respect that the experiences of Austria should be examined.

ANNEX

LIST OF PARTICIPANTS
IN THE MULTINATIONAL STUDY GROUP

Canada

Mr. Peter Bartha,
Economic Consultant,
The Canadian Manufacturers' Association

Mr. Russel Bell,
Research Director,
Canadian Labour Congress

Mr. Allan Porter,
Chief, Wages Research Division
Department of Labour

Finland

Mr. Nils Nilsson,
Secretary for Economic Research,
Central Organisation of Finnish Trade Unions

Mr. Tauno Ranta,
Director,
Finnish Employers' Confederation

Ireland

Mr. Maurice P. Cosgrave,
General Secretary,
Post Office Workers' Union

Mr. Charles Cuffe,
Director General,
Federated Union of Employers

Ireland (cont'd)

Mr. Tadhg O'Carroll,
Secretary-General,
Department of Labour

Netherlands

Mr. B. J. Van Enst,
Wage-Policy and Social Economic Policy Department,
Federation of Netherlands Industry

Mr. G. J. Van der Hoeven,
Economic Adviser,
Netherlands Confederation of Trade Unions (NVV)

United Kingdom

Mr. Roger James Dawe,
Principal,
Prices and Incomes Division, Department of Employment

Mr. Patrick Fisher,
Secretary, Production Department,
Trades Union Congress

Mr. Edward Robertson,
Director of Research,
Engineering Employers' Federation

Consultant

Co-chairman and Rapporteur:

Mr. Derek Robinson,
Oxford University Institute of Statistics and Economics,
Fellow of Magdalen College

OECD

Chairman:

Dr. Friedrich Klau,
Head of Country Studies Division - III
Economics and Statistics Department

Mr. Oliver Clarke,
Administrator in charge of Industrial Relations,
Manpower and Social Affairs Directorate

PROGRAMME OF THE STUDY GROUP

Monday 30th November

Morning   Opening statements by Austrian government personalities.

Introduction on the quantitative aspects of the Austrian economy by Professor Seidel of the Economic Research Institute (WFI).

Industrial relations and incomes policy in Austria.

Short introductory speech given by Dr. Vester of the Federal Chamber of Trade and Industry, Vienna.

Followed by discussion with representatives of the competent government authorities, the social partners and research institutes.

Afternoon   Joint Commission on Prices and Incomes (short introductory speech and then discussion with members of this Commission about the origin, development, structure, functions, links with administration, government and academic community, fields of action, especially with respect to the price and wage regulations of the "Beirat").

The Prices and Wages Sub-Committees (short introductory speech by representatives of the Sub-Committees followed by discussion).

Attended by Dr. Heinz Kienzl (Deputy Director General of the Austrian National Bank), Dr. Thomas Lachs (Head of the Economic Policy Department of the OGB) and representatives of the Trade Unions and Chamber of Commerce.

Tuesday, 1st December

Morning Price and wage determination in two selected branches: food processing and metal industries. Specific cases of wage fixing and price fixing – beer price, price of foundry products.

Discussion with representatives of the Trade Unions, Austrian Federation of Industry and Commerce.

Afternoon Three separate discussion groups:

  i) Trade Union
  ii) Employer
  iii) Governmental

Wednesday, 2nd December

Morning Visit to the firm of Grundmann, Herzogenberg, and discussions.

Afternoon Visit to the Brewery Schwechat.

Thursday, 3rd December

Morning Meeting of participants and OECD representatives.

Afternoon Austrian Price and Wage Policy from the general economic point of view.

(Discussion with experts from the WFI and the Federal Chamber of Commerce, the Chamber of Labour and other competent experts).

Friday, 4th December

Morning Role of the Joint Commission on Prices and Wages for stability, economic growth, income distribution and social peace from the viewpoint of the Austrian governmen

-----

Afternoon Round table discussion, followed by full discussion with representatives of the government and social partners, research people.

If the Austrian Price and Wage Policy is a success, what are the reasons and what lessons can other countries draw from it.

OECD SALES AGENTS
DEPOSITAIRES DES PUBLICATIONS DE L'OCDE

OECD PUBLICATIONS, 2, rue André-Pascal, 75775 Paris Cedex 16 - No. 30.877 1972

PRINTED IN FRANCE